The [illegible]

Jennif[illegible]'s Diary by One Fat Lady

By Jennifer Paterson

Illustrated by Robert Geary

Oldie Publications Ltd
London

This compilation first published by
Oldie Publications Ltd

The publishers would like to thank the respective copyright owners
for permission to include material in this volume

A CIP catalogue record for this book is available from
The British Library

Distribution by
World Leisure Marketing, 9 Downing Road,
West Meadows Industrial Estate, Derby DE21 6HA.
Tel: 01332 343332

ISBN 1-9011700-05-5

Cover illustration by Robert Geary
Design & production Richard Adams Associates
Text printed and bound by Woolnough Bookbinding Ltd
Covers printed by Amica Fine Art Print Ltd

Acknowledgements
Thanks to Richard Ingrams, James Pembroke, Marie Hemming, Rory Campbell,
Caroline Law, Richard Adams, Anne Clark, Sam Adams and all at WLM.

To Richard Ingrams and family -
Fred, Jubby, Otis, Queenie, Phoebe, Sam and Lily -
because I love them all; and to oldies everywhere.

Contents

Meat

Fish

Vegetarian

Side Dishes & Vegetables

Puddings & Cakes

Drinks

20 March 1992

WE HAD A most marvellous and moving requiem mass for my beloved uncle, the good canon, Monsignor Francis Bartlett. A huge procession of clergy headed by Cardinal Hume, six bishops, countless Monsignors with the faithful Gilbey at the helm (canons to the right and canons to the left plus about a hundred priests from various parishes), all came to mourn for a person they seemed genuinely to love for his wit and sense of humour as much as his excellent priestly qualities, as did the many friends who completely filled Westminster Cathedral. I was stunned.

We bore him off 'to paradise by way of Kensal Green', where he was buried in a nice grave by a tree. He was always very fond of good food and wine and was often found stirring up little Italian messes with Monsignor Pilkington during their days together at the cathedral. We shall miss him a lot.

Thinking of these little cook-ups reminds me that time-honoured Ingrams, a grandfather yet again, was asking for ideas for the lone eater who frankly can't or won't cook properly at home. As he seems to exist on fish fingers and baked beans I suggested he might at least make a good *sauce tartare*:

Pound three hard egg yolks with a tablespoon of Dijon mustard and a pinch of salt until very smooth, then add about half a pint of olive oil, drop by drop to start with, beating with a wooden spoon until it thickens. Then you can dribble the oil in more generously, thinning the sauce when necessary with a little lemon juice or wine vinegar. Chop finely three tablespoons each of capers, gherkins and fresh green herbs (parsley, chives, tarragon) and mix into the sauce. If truly lazy, use bought mayonnaise then add the goodies.

Another thing. Baked beans in tomato sauce are not the only beans in tins. There are delicious flageolets, red kidney, barlotti, haricots and cannellini. All these, drained, seasoned with lots of fresh ground pepper, salt, lemon juice and a few thin slices of onion, and dressed with good olive oil, are infinitely more delicious — though I know many people adore the old baked beans even eaten cold from the tin.

Have plenty of different shaped pastas in your cupboard. Buy De Cecco pasta from some good Italian shop. It is one of the best I know — penne, large or small, fedelini, which is the best size of spaghetti (rather fine and cooks in six minutes) — there are lots to choose from. A good hunk of Parmesan cheese, well wrapped in greaseproof paper and a plastic bag will keep for ages in the salad drawer of a refrigerator. Buy anchovies in a jar. Then you can take out one or two at will for a Scotch Woodcock (scrambled eggs on toast with anchovies crossed on top) or various additions to sauces.

Hang a whole salami in a cool place — always good for a munch, finely sliced. There are much better stock cubes now. Just Bouillon have an excellent new range with no monosodium or artificial flavours — chicken, beef, vegetable, onion, fish stock and court bouillon to cook fish in. I am going to live on them for Lent.

Some very good jars of antipasto have appeared on my Sainsbury's shelves called Sacla: wild mushrooms, pimentos, mixed artichokes and raw vegetables, mixed beans, all preserved in oil and spices — a very good addition to a simple slice of ham or chicken. There are also green and red pesto sauces which can be added to mashed potatoes, soups and pasta.

Try to have good bread. Cut it and keep in the deep freeze. Then you can take out your requirements for the day instead of finding old mouldy bits lying at the bottom of the bin. Potted shrimps are another standby to keep in the freezer. Cook them gently with eggs and cream or just with toast. Always have a supply of lemons. They too can be kept in the salad drawer of the fridge. I hope this is all a bit of a help.

17 April 1992

TODAY, THE WEDNESDAY before Easter, is called Spy Wednesday because it was the day that the treacherous Judas conspired with the chief priests and the elders to betray Jesus and deliver Him into their grubby hands. Holy or Maundy Thursday has a moment of joyous respite, being the commemoration of the institution of the Eucharist — the Maundy refers to the washing of the feet of the apostles. There is also something called 'maundy money', a silver-coin dole traditionally handed out on this day by the royal almoner.

At Westminster Cathedral the Cardinal washes the feet of the splendid Chelsea pensioners. Good Friday requires fasting and abstinence, the fast being broken by some good fish dish in the evening, and is probably the best day for fishmongers in the whole year. Fish pie is a great favourite with nearly everybody but fish pudding is rarely seen in England and is quite delicious. Herewith:

Lou's Norwegian Fish Pudding

8 oz of proper smoked haddock (undyed)
8 oz of smoked cod
6 fluid oz of double cream
$1^1/_2$ tablespoons of potato flour
10 fluid oz of milk
2 teaspoons of salt
Freshly-ground black pepper

For the sauce
1 oz of butter
1 oz of plain flour
12 fluid oz of milk
3 teaspoons of tomato purée
2 tablespoons of sherry
Juice of half a lemon
3 oz of smoked mussels
3 oz of smoked oysters or 8 oz of peeled shrimps

You can make this pudding in a three-pint ring mould or six individual timbals. Skin the fish, place it in a food processor and whizz for a few seconds. Alternatively, mince or chop very finely. Add the milk, cream, potato flour, salt and a good grinding of pepper. Whizz again. Put the mixture into the lightly-oiled mould or timbals. Cover with kitchen foil. Place in a roasting tin half-filled with water and bake in a preheated oven at Gas 6, 400 F, 200 C, for about 20 minutes until firm to the touch. While this is going on, prepare the sauce. Melt the butter in a saucepan and add the flour to make a roux, then gradually add the warmed milk stirring all the time to avoid lumps. Add the tomato purée, sherry and lemon juice to taste. Bring to simmering point and cook for another 15 minutes. Check the seasoning. Add the smoked oysters and mussels or peeled shrimps. Let them heat through but on no account let them boil. When the pudding is cooked, ease around the edges of the mould with a sharp knife. Place the serving-dish on top of the mould, turn it upside down quickly, give it a shake from right to left and it should plop on to the dish. Pour the sauce over the pudding, sprinkle a little chopped parsley and decorate with some unpeeled shrimps. Serve immediately with a watercress salad.

I think Lou of the Norwegian Fish Pudding was the grandmother of Roald Dahl of blessed memory. He was intensely interested in food and a good cook himself.

Now a festive pudding for Easter made from chocolate and eggs, which I got from the beautiful Mirana Colvin:

Chocomousse

6 oz of very good plain chocolate — Menier
6 oz of unsalted butter
4 oz of sugar
4 eggs
10 small dariole moulds, greased and floured

Melt the chocolate and butter over a pan of simmering water. Beat the egg yolks and sugar until creamy and hanging like ribbons from the beater. Mix with the chocolate and allow to cool. Beat the egg whites stiffly and gently fold into the chocolate mixture. Pour or ladle into the dariole moulds and bake on tray in a pre-heated hot oven at Gas 8, 450 F or 230 C for 10 to 15 minutes. Turn out while still hot, to hold their shape better. Leave to cool and dust with icing sugar.

You could serve this together with whipped cream or a butterscotch or chocolate sauce, or even a real custard if you like it — I don't. If you have no moulds I imagine a greased loaf or cake-tin would do, but it would not look as charming.

1 May 1992

I WENT TO two election parties where I broke my Lenten intention of not drinking, with the consequence that my alcohol-free system has produced the grandpappy of all hangovers. I feel like darling Jeff Bernard looks but with a hatchet stuck in the middle of my head for decoration.

Other excitements of the week included a splendidly entertaining *Evening Standard* literary lunch given at the Café Royal. Among the stars was Mrs Edna Healey, who has just written a book about Coutts and Co. AN Wilson, who hosted the whole thing most charmingly, said it was a fascinating book but that Edna Healey's speech was rather boring. John Mortimer was pushing his *Dunster* and was his usual benign and very hilarious socialist self, but the out-and-out shining performer was our beloved and brilliant Beryl Bainbridge, who had everyone convulsed with laughter and weeping in the aisles after a superb rendering from her incredible *The Birthday Boys*. The food was by Forte. Enough said.

We all know about defrosted prawns and the ubiquitous prawn cocktail, which was served as our first course, but this one went into nightmare fantasyland by being garnished with slices of tinned peaches. Who could have thought that one up? The terrible pink sauce that always comes with this famous delicacy can very easily be replaced by whipped cream flavoured with tomato purée, lemon juice, salt and a pinch of cayenne pepper — easy and delicious. However, the whole event was a great success. I didn't realise so many people went to these affairs.

Owing to the lack of anything else in the larder I recently made a rather good little dish you might like to try. I had some old sour cream and mushrooms that needed using up, plus a pork fillet. Cook the sliced mushrooms (about $^1/_4$ of a pound) in butter in a frying-pan, add $^1/_4$ pint of sour cream, salt, lots of ground pepper and grated nutmeg. Let it come to bubbling point, stirring all together. Slice the pork fillet into thinnish rounds and stir-fry rapidly in a well-heated heavy pan, using a little olive-oil. When cooked through, season with salt, pepper, a sprinkling of chopped parsley and a squeeze of lemon juice, mix with the mushroom sauce, adjust seasoning and serve with some plain boiled rice and whatever vegetables you have to hand. Young turnips are in the market now and are ideal with their succulent peppery flavour.

15 May 1992

IT WAS SIR Arthur Sullivan's birthday last week. Born in 1842, his only legacy to dishes of the time that I can find include: Mikado ('exalted gate') Consommé: chicken broth and fresh tomato juice; Mikado Noisettes of Beef or Lamb, (fried in butter and seated on half a tomato with buttered artichokes); and Mikado salad — young chrysanthemum leaves, sliced cold potatoes, artichoke bottoms, prawns, capers and beetroot doused in vinaigrette. I hate beetroot leaking its blood over everything in a salad. The best thing to do with it is bake it in its skin like a potato, split it open and pile with sour cream and mint, delicious with slices of cold meat or poultry.

I had a novel mishap this week. My loyal motor-bike, which is part of my bloodstream, blew a gasket. However, it gamely limped in to my saviours at Scootabout who did what was necessary, but it left me to come home on a bus which I don't think I have done for at least two years. I airily produced my old-age card; to no avail as it was out of date. How can old age be out of date? I had to take my passport and driving licence to the post office to prove I had not returned to gilded youth. Only then was I given a new card, which I suppose I won't use again until it meets the same fate. At least my bike hasn't been stolen yet. Poor Father Ronald at the London Oratory had his moped stolen from the very same precinct, locked though it was.

There is always something exciting going on at church: music, new people, old friends and any church worth its salt has some wonderful loonies to amuse and terrify you. We had a splendid woman in last month who stalked up to the altar in the middle of a Haydn mass and emptied onto the steps the contents of a carrier bag: a lot of dog-meat tins and pints of milk. She then marched back down the centre aisle yelling in some foreign tongue. What child could ask for more? Everyone behaved as though nothing had happened and the great sacristan, Mr Trimmer, removed the evidence with quiet dignity and a mop. After your prayers and conversations with The Almighty you can go and have the largest martini in the world and feel it well deserved. Try this for a nice little Sunday lunch which will take an hour to cook on your return home. Do the stuffing the night before.

Guinea Fowl

Fry 3 oz of diced bacon and 4 oz of chopped shallots in olive-oil until browning. Add the chopped bird's or chicken's liver. Cook for a minute. Add 3 oz of chopped black olives and a teaspoon of thyme. Season. Mix all together and stuff into the bird's cavity. Anoint the bird with olive-oil and cook in a pre-heated oven for 45 minutes at Gas 7, 425F, 218C. Baste every 20 minutes while you are sipping your cocktails and serve with the easiest and most succulent vegetables you can manage. I had very good frozen roast potatoes at Anna Haycraft's table. A doddle with a little rosemary strewn about them.

29 May 1992

NO ONE SHOULD pay the slightest bit of attention to diet literature. When people still ate at normal meal-times, you ate what was put in front of you, with treats for high-days and holidays. Everyone was healthy without delving into things like calories and fibres. There is a Frenchman over here with another book about getting thin eating what you like. He nevertheless gives a harsh list of forbidden foods, and instructs us to 'wait five hours after a lipidic meal before consuming any carbohydrates.' Apparently the French eat cheese and do little exercise, but enjoy a level of cholesterol on a par with the Japanese. Well, I have yet to meet a French person who isn't suffering from a *crise.* I also get outrageous newsletters from the Chocolate Society telling me where to buy the richest chocolates.

A lunch with Willie Landels this week included two dishes I had never had before, both quite exquisite though very simple.

Milan Risotto

For 3 to 4 people:
12 oz Italian arborio rice
2 tbs olive oil
1 medium size red onion, finely chopped
1.5 pints hot vegetable stock
2 tbs freshly grated Parmesan
1 tbs minutely chopped, fresh rosemary
1 dessert spoon grated lemon peel

Fry the onion in oil until softened. Add the rice and stir for about 2 minutes over a brisk heat. Pour half a pint of the hot stock into the rice and add the rosemary. Stir and simmer gently until the stock is absorbed. Add further 1/4 pints of the stock every 3 to 4 minutes until it is all absorbed. Keep stirring every now and then to avoid the rice sticking to the pan. The total cooking time should be about 25 minutes. The rice should look creamy, rather like sloppy porridge, but still have a bite to it. Season with salt, pepper and the lemon peel. Stir in the Parmesan cheese. Add a few cooked peas for colour if you like. Let it rest for 2 minutes then serve. The taste of the lemon peel and rosemary is enchanting and fresh.

Green Artichoke Salad

This is tricky but worthwhile. Peel the leaves off the artichokes until you come to the purple and pale green part. Discard the hard green leaves. Cut into quarters and remove the chokes. Cut the remaining quarters into fine slices vertically and plunge them into a basin of cold water or they will discolour. Fry some chopped garlic in 3 tablespoons of olive oil. Drain the artichokes, pat dry and stir into the pan. Moisten with a glass of white wine and cook over a good heat for 10 minutes. Season. Pour into a receptacle and cool.

I had a perfect Eggs Benedict at Simply Nico yesterday. Along with the usual ingredients, the eggs were placed on a *duxelles* of chopped mushrooms and shallots fried in butter. This is always a delicious mixture and a very good bed to lie grilled chicken or turkey breasts upon as they can be rather dry. Hollandaise is good with practically everything. *Vive les diets.*

12 June 1992

I HAVE JUST had one of England's perfect-weather weekends in the country with my dear friend Professor John Martin Robinson, he who protects our houses and heritage. He was a wonderful host, the guests were charming, the countryside was *en beauté*, but getting there and back was a nightmare ending in disaster. Good old British Rail got us to Lancaster an hour late; first the overhead cables went, then the signals were on fire so we had to crawl from stop to signal to avoid a train crash, and to top it all we had to make an unscheduled stop at Nuneaton to expel an unruly passenger (a fighting drunk Scotsman). The return journey was only half an hour late but not without incident. This time it was a fighting drunk Scottish lass careering down the aisles waving a flat iron and screaming vile abuse at her fleeing lover. Where did she get the iron from? Having docked into Euston with a sigh of relief and longing for home and bed, the worst was to come. I found my trusty motorcycle and its surrounding companions had been put to the torch by some fiends. There she was, all blackened with dripping trails of black rubber – so sad.

On to happier things. I had a letter from one Diana Hall, who I see lives round the corner from me, offering her receipt from an old 1929 cookery book for 'real' Scotch Woodcock as opposed to scrambled eggs crossed with anchovies.

Diana Hall's Scotch Woodcock

3-4 slices of toast
3 egg yolks
5 anchovies
$^1/_2$ pint of cream or milk
Salt and pepper

Cut very thin toast into fingers and butter them. Wash, scrape, bone and chop the anchovies finely. Put them on the toast. Beat up the yolks of the eggs with the milk or cream. Season well with freshly ground pepper and salt (remembering the saltiness of the anchovies). Cook over a low heat stirring all the time until the eggs thicken, but do not let them boil. Arrange the anchovy toast on a hot dish and pour the egg mixture over. Very good I'm sure, especially when made with cream, a sort of savoury custard, quite different to Arabella Boxer's version in her book of English food:

Arabella Boxer's Scotch Woodcock

8 anchovy fillets
16 capers
4 thick slices of dry white bread, crusts removed
6 whole eggs
1 oz of butter
4 tablespoons of milk
Sea-salt and black pepper

Soak the anchovy fillets in the milk for 10 minutes, rinse under the cold tap and pat dry. Rinse the capers in a small strainer and pat dry. Toast the bread and cut into neat 2-inch squares. Spread them with half the butter and keep warm. Beat the eggs, adding sea-salt and black pepper then scramble as usual in the remaining butter. Pile onto the squares of toast and lay the anchovy fillets crosswise over the top, placing a caper between each angle. Serve immediately. Serves 4 as a savoury or 2 as a first course on larger pieces of toast.

Congratulations to Arabella Boxer for winning the Glenfiddich Award last week.

What next? The elephant garlic from Chile is about to stampede into our lives. They can be eight times the size of an ordinary garlic bulb with a much milder and sweeter taste, rather like a leek. It can be eaten raw and finely sliced in sandwiches and salads — must be awfully healthy. It has about five or six huge cloves and would be splendid for that chicken dish roasted with 40 cloves of normal garlic. Roast the chicken on a bed of garlic moistened with wine and annointed with butter. The result is perfectly delicious and the garlic becomes sweet, mild and somewhat caramelised. I have found some of these jumbo bulbs at Safeways.

My last tip is a speedy soup to knock up for unexpected guests, as we were over the weekend to Sal Sharp of Linden Hall. Whizz tinned tomatoes and bottled (or real if you have it) beetroot together, season and serve with a dollop of sour cream and a sprinkling of some green herb. Can be hot or cold. Beautiful colour and taste.

26 June 1992

WHAT A SAD end to a glorious May — the death of the great and illustrious Elizabeth David. I owe her an enormous debt of gratitude, as I'm sure many of us oldies do, not to mention future generations who will be inspired by her books forever, I hope. Her descriptions of cooking and eating should be a joy for any beginner. God rest her soul and supply her with endless heavenly delights.

I went to the opening of the enlarged dear old San Martino in Walton Street last week. I also went to the original opening, when it was in the hands of two nice young men, Tim Page and Norman Parkinson's son. That, I found to my horror, was 22 years ago. Martino seems just the same and is still producing his famous Spaghetti San Martino cooked in a paper bag with a wonderfully fragrant seafood sauce. We were given great steaming bowls of it and as usual it was perfect. He is a dear man and together with his enchanting wife runs a good, honest restaurant, growing most of his vegetables in his garden in Tooting. I like that.

During the heat I have been trying to prepare food in the coolth of the morning. I've made what turns out to be a most delicious and charming-looking jellied rabbit.

Jellied Rabbit

It is essential to have a good jellied chicken or meat stock for this. I collect bones in the freezer until there are enough to make a good amount of stock. Boil them with an onion, a couple of carrots, a bay leaf and parsley stalks for about an hour. Season, strain, cool, chill, then remove the solidified fat. Hey presto, lovely jellied stock. A split pig's trotter added to the bones produces a really stiff jelly.

I used a large packet of Sainsbury's farmed rabbit. Remove any obvious bits of fat. With enough stock to cover the meat, bring to the boil. Add about 3 to 4 tablespoons of dry vermouth, drop the rabbit pieces in together with some prepared and sliced baby carrots, turn the heat down and poach gently until the meat is tender, about half an hour. Remove the rabbit and carrots with a slotted spoon, leave to cool a bit, then remove the flesh from the bones. Cool the stock enough to remove any surplus fat. Cut the meat into healthy chunks and return it to the stock. Add the carrots. Strain 2 oz of capers and chop together with a goodly amount of parsley, chives and tarragon or marjoram or what you will. Stir well into the rabbit mixture. Pour the whole lot into a dainty mould and chill until set. Turn out onto a plate, decorate with fillets of anchovies and some quarters of hardboiled eggs, or, even better, whole quails' eggs.

Serve with a potato salad heavily impregnated with Dijon mustard and maybe a tomato salad on the side. This looks delightful and is a highly suitable summer supper dish.

24 July 1992

I HAD THE unusual honour last week of being godmother, or sponsor as they now call it, to the excellent Humphry Berkeley on the occasion of his confirmation by Bishop Crowley at the London Oratory. Unusual, as Humphry is 66. He was christened into the Catholic faith when up at Cambridge by the admirable Monsignor Alfred Gilbey about 40 years ago, but life being what it is, confirmation was somehow forgotten. However, the matter has now been put to rights with the now venerable Monsignor, still splendid, in attendance. Humphry Berkeley wrote a really funny book while at Cambridge, where he was President of the Union, called *The Life and Death of Rochester Sneath*, a collection of letters of devastating accuracy, parodying the public school system. G B Shaw was puzzled, Ronald Knox helpful, the Master of Marlborough exasperated, the headmaster of St Benedict's livid etc, etc. After Sneath had been revealed as Berkeley, he was rusticated and forbidden his college for two years. Such spoilsports. I remember an article of his describing his kidnapping in Africa by ferocious blacks who bundled him into the boot of a car then got him out to shoot him in the head. He survived by telling them they were very wicked men and giving them a blessing. They were so taken aback they let him go free. A remarkable fellow.

During one of these boiling hot days I was invited to lunch at the Cadogan Hotel hard on the heels of John Osborne, though I did not spy him there. It was lovely nonetheless. I can't remember when I last visited it but it is now part of the Historic House Hotels and is looking charming. Lots of room, airy, a good bar in a comfortable country house-type room and good service. No hurry or scurry and a perfectly delicious set lunch including a half bottle of house wine for £15.50, not bad, eh? The main course changes each day and there are a selection of starters and puddings to choose from. I was there on a Monday and started with salad leaves dressed with chicken livers and pistachio, followed by Escallop of Pork Holstein, tender as a baby's bottom, with well-cooked vegetables, and a pretty strawberry Bavarois in a red fruit sauce. The taste was fine but as is so often the case it was far too solidified with gelatine; you could have thrown it against the wall and caught it on the rebound. A lemon tart with raspberries was adjudged great. All in all a very nice place to meet, eat or drink. Kind staff is always a bonus.

Yesterday I made that most exquisite of summer puddings which you never get in restaurants, or if you do it is too smooth.

Gooseberry Fool

The gooseberry season is not very long so rush out and buy some. Puréed, they can be frozen for the winter. For the Fool, top and tail 1lb of green gooseberries, rinse under cold water. Place in a saucepan with 2oz of unsalted butter and stew gently with the lid on until just cooked, not for very long, about 5 to 10 minutes. Mash with a silver or wooden fork, sweeten to taste (I use 5-6oz of sugar), allow to cool then fold into a half pint of thick cream whipped until it forms peaks. Pour into a ravishing glass bowl, or, if you prefer, individual, dainty bowls. Chill well and serve with ratafia or amoretti biscuits. If you delete the sugar, this same mixture goes wonderfully well with grilled or smoked mackerel. Some people like a little sugar added but I add a teaspoon or so of crushed fennel seeds which produces a very good flavour, unless, that is, you are one of those who detest fennel.

Tomato and Rice Salad

Make with those fragrant wine tomatoes which are about. Marvellous with cold chicken or meat. Skin 6 tomatoes, slice and lay on a plate, sprinkle with salt and pepper. Boil 8oz of good rice for about 12 minutes to retain a little bite. Drain and dress immediately with salt, pepper, nutmeg, 4 tablespoons of virgin olive oil and 2 teaspoons of tarragon vinegar. Mix thoroughly, place in a suitable, longish dish, cover with the tomatoes, sprinkle with a good chopping of chives, tarragon and finely cut parsley and leave to cool. The juices from the tomatoes will soak into the rice and be a delight to the consumer. I use the Italian arborio rice for this dish as it soaks up the flavours so well.

7 August 1992

WHAT A LOT of hoo-hah went on about the Garrick Club restricting its membership to men. It seemed to be much more important than anything going on in Parliament. I am delighted that it remains a men's club and can't understand these women who want to become members. If men have a club they cherish and love, why shouldn't they? It's their club and their vote. It's very kind of them to allow us there as guests. I love being taken there. I love the secret staircase we females have to ascend in order not to desecrate the male Tom Tiddler's ground. From top to bottom it is covered with fascinating pictures of theatrical persons of yesteryear, and I could spend hours loitering there without intent. Also, there is one of the most charming ladies' rooms in London, a little bower of hospitality. I don't know any women who want to join men's clubs but if women want a club, they must make one of their own, starting with the acquisition of some historic building. A good place for such a thing might be the soon-to-close Elizabeth Garrett Anderson Hospital for Women. Or better still, unite and help it to continue.

Last week a friend, who has a splendid job which includes taking foreigners to Glyndebourne, asked me for suggestions for a really English dish to take for the picnic, having done all the smoked or fresh salmon bit before. He thought brawn but I reckoned it would wobble itself to death on the journey and might be a touch too daring for the foreign guests. I plumped for a cold leg of the best lamb, which cannot be bettered in its own class. I bought a beautiful leg last week from Sainsbury's – the sort that heralds from contented sheep and idyllic pastures.

Cold Leg of Contented Lamb

Caress the whole leg with good olive oil. Slice a garlic clove into tiny slithers and insert just under the skin and into the bone edges. Place on a rack in an oven tin. Pour some water in the bottom of the tin. Season the skin with ground salt and pepper. Place some branches of rosemary above and below. Cook in a pre-heated oven at Gas 9, 470°F, 243°C, for 15 minutes, then lower the heat to Gas 4, 355°F, 179°C, for the rest of the cooking, which should be 15 minutes per pound plus another 15 minutes in all. Remove from the oven and leave to cool thoroughly. If taking it to Glyndebourne, wrap in several sheets of grease-proof paper. I hate vinegar but love mint, so I make a good

mayonnaise and add a great deal of chopped mint. This makes a gorgeous and exciting sauce for the cold pink lamb. Together with a salad of new Jersey potatoes and some little broad beans dressed with oil and lemon, what foreigner could ask for a more English repast. To follow you could have:

Melon Stuffed with Raspberries

Strew 1lb of raspberries with castor sugar then pour a small glass of Grand Marnier or the like over them. Leave for a few hours to infuse. Cut a slice off the top of a medium-size melon. Scoop out the flesh and discard the seeds. Chop the flesh and mix with the raspberries. Pile the lot back into the melon skin. Put the lid back on and fasten with Scotch tape. Place in a good plastic bag, secure firmly, then chill. As well as guarding against seepage, the bag will prevent the scent of the melon pervading everything in the refrigerator.

I wish someone had taken me to Glyndebourne, but it seems you can get in only if you know a friendly bank nowadays.

21 August 1992

I HAVE HAD another jolly jaunt by train to Peterborough from Kings Cross, a better class of station than Euston. The journey was over in a trice and very comfortable but there was yet another very drunk Scotsman aboard swearing violently at the charming guard who had a most beautiful voice when intoning his welcomes. Does everyone find a drunk on the train?

I was going to visit a Loch Fyne oyster bar at Elton with my friend John Noble. He lives on Loch Fyne where he started his first smoke-house and oyster bar in a disused cattle byre: he now has one in Nottingham. Elton is his latest conversion, at grand Elton House. Imagine a large platter of fresh oysters, a dressed crab in its shell, mussels, crab claws, langoustines and ravishing little queen scallops – all for £10.95, amazing.

There is every form of smoked fish, wonderful pale cured kippers and haddock, as well as the excellent salmon which they have in the normal cold smoke fashion or by a new method which produced Bradhan Ròst, which is Gaelic for roasted salmon, but it isn't. It is hot smoked using a little peat and ends up looking more like cooked salmon and is cut vertically in thick slices. I wouldn't say I prefer it to the usual smoked salmon but it is an interesting alternative. It is served hot or cold with a sauce of horseradish, crème fraiche and a drop of malt whisky.

All these delicacies from Loch Fyne, including smoked venison I think, can be ordered and delivered overnight. Get the list from Clachan Farm, Arkinglas, Cairndow, Argyll PA26 8BH.

For those who can't do without their chocolate fix here is an iced drink to tempt the strongest wills. From the Chocolate Society we have 'Chocolate L'Ancienne', perfect for a lazy, hot afternoon.

'Chocolate L'Ancienne'

For four people you need

6 oz of the best plain chocolate with at least 61% cocoa content (see wrapper)
17 fluid oz of full cream milk
4 fluid oz of water
a small pinch of salt

2 rounded dessertspoons castor sugar, 1 cup (8 fluid oz I reckon) of espresso or very strong coffee

4 oz of rum.

For the topping:

2 ice cubes

5 fluid oz of double cream

4 fluid oz of milk

3 dessertspoons of castor sugar

Break the chocolate into small pieces and place in a pan with the salt and water. Melt over a very low heat stirring all the time, don't let it boil, just melt. Use a bain-marie if you prefer. When the chocolate is smooth and shiny add the milk little by little then the sugar. Bring to the boil and simmer for 5 minutes. Take care as at this moment the chocolate rises and thickens rapidly. Add the rum and coffee and boil for a further 2 minutes. Allow to cool, then chill. For the topping, put the ice cubes into a bowl, add the cream, milk and sugar. Whip with an electric beater until stiff. Chill. To assemble, beat the chocolate with a whisk to lighten it, pour into suitable glasses and top with the whipped cream and some grated chocolate. This wonderful drink was served to the court audience in the inner sanctum of performances by 'Mozart au Chocolat', a troupe of French performers.

4 September 1992

VERY UNUSUAL HAPPENINGS this past week, hardly credible. A 28-stone woman killed her rival by sitting on her. One wonders who the brave man worth killing for is, and how he compels such devotion from this weighty lass. A couple returning rather merrily from a wedding had congress in a second-class compartment of a train in full view of the other passengers, who only complained when they lit up a post-coital cigarette. The compartment was a non-smoker, as they all are now except for one carriage right at the end where you find a much better class of people reading much better literature, and what is more it is uncrowded compared to the rest of the sardine-packed train.

To crown it all, these male homosexual nuns arrived at Westminster Cathedral to picket the Piazza and disturb the sung High Mass. Then about 50 of them rose and produced banners against the Pope. One old lady in a wheelchair passed out in fright and had to be resuscitated and comforted, poor old thing. I do think it was very ill-mannered of these silly queens and not the best way to plead their cause.

Rice Balls

You don't often come across rice balls served in this country. They are perfectly delicious and a good way to use up the remains of a risotto, or can be made from scratch using the following method. This will make about 26 balls, so you can halve or quarter the amounts to suit yourself.

For the sauce, fry 1lb of good beef mince in a non-stick pan, turning all the time until lightly browned. Drain off any fat or liquid that accumulates. Finely chop 2 onions, 2 carrots and one stick of celery and fry in 4fl oz of olive oil quite gently until soft and barely golden (use a saucepan). Add paprika to taste, the cooked meat, 4oz of frozen peas and a generous pint of home-made tomato sauce. Simmer for about 45 minutes until thickened. Adjust seasoning and cool.

To make the risotto, have 5 pints of beef stock on the simmer. Melt 6oz of butter in a large saucepan. Add 2lbs of Arborio rice, stirring until well cooked. Add the beef stock ladle by ladle, waiting until each is absorbed before adding the next. After 10 minutes, put 10 threads of saffron into the rice and continue cooking until it is smooth and creamy with an *al dente* consistency. You may not need all the stock. Add a further 2oz of butter and 2oz of freshly grated Parmesan cheese. Mix well, turn the rice out into a large bowl, cool a bit then beat in 2 large eggs.

Make the rice balls while the rice is still warm as it is easier that way. Pour 4oz of fine breadcrumbs into a soup bowl, and set out the cooled meat sauce. Wet your hands and shape the rice in a cupped hand, making an indentation in the centre to form a well. Transfer a dessertspoon of the sauce into the well then cover with more rice to form a ball about the size of a small tangerine. Roll each ball in the breadcrumbs and set aside until you have used up all the rice.

Heat 3 inches of vegetable oil in a frier or a saucepan until a cube of bread frizzles golden quite quickly. Fry the rice balls, turning them in the oil until evenly cooked, crisp and golden brown – about 3 minutes. To test, insert a skewer, remove it and feel if it is warm to the touch. Keep the cooked balls hot in the oven on some kitchen towel to drain whilst you cook the rest, as I suppose you will need to do them in batches. Serve piping hot. If you are not into meat sauce, replace the sauce with a cube of mozzarella in the centre of the ball. Very good either way.

18 September 1992

NO GREAT HAZARDS on my bus trip to Cumberland except for eternal delays on the highway due to roadworks. Once we settled into our seats it proved very pleasant. My companion, Tom Hartman, has become devoted to the bus trip since the confiscation of his driving licence. One sits nice and high with an excellent view of the countryside. There was a very dramatic moment on a road overlooking a valley when two of those dangerous but beautiful jets whooshed by beneath us.

I took a perfect little picnic to avoid the ghastly sandwiches on sale. We had pink vodka cocktails on the rocks, generous smoked salmon sandwiches, followed by those little roast quail – which are an excellent picnic food – a box of cherry tomatoes and nectarines washed down with red wine – a wholesome repast to while away the time. The people in the adjacent seats were eating something quite terrible-looking from aircraft trays. The fare was £32.50 return to Carlisle which is incredibly good value. The one annoying innovation is that you don't get seat numbers any more. Going down was all right as we secured our seats at Victoria but on the return trip there were no double seats so we had to travel apart for half the journey, which was ridiculous. Also on the way back they kept announcing that the drinking of alcohol on the bus was a punishable offence. Why? All the passengers seemed deeply respectable – not a hooligan or train drunk in sight.

Back at my beloved market in Tatchbrook Street, Victoria, my splendid greengrocer Fred Foster had a new treat on display: wonderful plaits of smoked garlic. They are pale kipper colour and have a terrific smell, but the smokiness is mostly in the skin. I tried them out with a couple of little poussins and, with a little help from the other ingredients, they were truly great.

Smoked Garlic Poussins

In a flame-proof casserole which will take two poussins fairly snugly, heat 6 tablespoons of olive oil. Put a tablespoon of olive paste and a squeeze of lemon into the cavities of the birds. Place them in the oil and brown on all sides. Add 10 fat cloves of the smoked garlic (if you can't find it never mind, use the ordinary), leaving the skins on. Fry for a moment or two. Pour in about 5 fl oz of dry vermouth. (I used Sainsbury's Italian which is reasonable and has a good flavour for cooking.) Season well with sea salt and freshly ground black pepper and tuck in a couple of fragrant bay leaves. Paint the little creatures with a liberal amount of Chinese black bean sauce. Cover and place in a pre-heated oven Gas 5, 380°F, 193°C for about 45 minutes or until tender, basting occasionally. A fine mixture of tastes from North, South, East and West. Good with plain rice.

Smoked Kippers

Remember the beautiful smoked kippers I received from Loch Fyne? They made a most delicious raw dish, so succulent they were. Find some, making sure they are not the dyed variety. Cut the tails off and skin. Remove the fillets from the bone and lay them in a shallow dish. Marinate in olive oil and lemon juice at a ratio of 1 spoon of juice to 6 of oil mixed with a good grinding of black pepper and a pinch of sugar. Make a potato salad with some good waxy potatoes – those little fir apples are perfect. Dress with the same vinaigrette adding some Dijon mustard and salt to taste. Chill the kipper fillets and serve surrounded by the potatoes. A sprinkling of dill and you have a dish for a king.

2 October 1992

I WENT TO a very strange event put on by the British Meat Information Service, held on the roof garden of Derry and Toms. I hadn't been there since childhood but the flamingoes were still there. This affair was meant to encourage meat-eating for Christmas rather than the tired old turkey (also not hung long enough any more). There were large pictures of various unknown 'celebrities' telling us what various joints of meat they were going to choose for their Christmas Dinner. I am sure she is a sweet and cuddly creature but I am really not the slightest bit interested or impressed by what Barbara Windsor (the only one I recognized) is munching on December 25th. We were lectured on these facts by an unspeakable little fellow (another 'celebrity' perhaps?) who chose to entertain us with questionable jokes and snide remarks about (guess who?) the royal family. The situation was eventually saved by the appearance of Rowley Leigh, the excellent chef from London's Kensington Place restaurant. Now he really does know his onions – or meat in this case – and proceeded to carve up great pieces of beef, lamb, pork and gammon. I love to see a master boning the carcass. He gave us this receipt:

Roast Rib Eye of British Beef with shallots, raspberry vinegar and red wine

1 forerib of beef, 8-10 lbs
1 lb of shallots
3 tsp raspberry vinegar
1 bottle of full-bodied red wine
salt and pepper

Remove the outside flap from the rib, which can be used later for mince or stew. Remove rib bones and any tough sinews and 'backstrap' from the top of the joint and tie up the meat into a roll (I should get your butcher to do all this). Place the beef on the bones into a roasting tin, season very well with salt and pepper and roast in a preheated oven at Gas 4-5, 180C, 350F for 20 minutes per pound plus 20 minutes for rare. I don't think I would give it that extra time. Let it rest somewhere warm for at least 15 minutes after cooking. Whilst the meat is cooking slice the shallots finely, cook and colour them in a little butter, add the vinegar and two thirds of the wine. Stew this mixture until it has reduced by half. When the meat and bones are removed from the pan, deglaze with the rest of the wine, add any juices from the joint and strain into the shallot and wine mixture. Season to taste. Serve thick slices of the roast covered with the sauce, roast potatoes, broccoli, french beans and carrots.

16 October 1992

I DO NOT approve of capital punishment for the simple reason that I would not like to be the executioner. But there are certain times when I would kill for pleasure. For example, yesterday, when all set to fly on my Honda broomstick, I found the spider straps which hold my basket on the back had been swiped by a malefactor leaving me with nothing to secure my goods and chattels. It was a Sunday too, and I was on my way to church – not a good time for murderous thoughts. However, on arrival at the Oratory I found poor Father Ronald had had another scooter stolen which put my complaints in the shade. Thus it always is.

I have been to a luncheon at the Café Royal where the British Team of Chefs for the Culinary Olympics in Frankfurt were displaying their wares for this year's competition. They are allowed to spend nine Deutschmarks a head, which is about £3 give or take a Bundesbank, so for once the food is in the realms of reality. None of your truffles and foie gras titbits here. There was Kensington Chicken Royal (a mousseline topped with black olives) and Beef Charterhouse (a smart boiled-beef-and-carrots affair). The meat was a disappointment, being smoked fillet instead of silverside. And for pudding, Bread and Butter Soufflé Victoria, which was excellent. So let us wish them well.

I have been trying out a rabbit receipt from Jeanne Strang's lovely book *Goose Fat and Garlic*, such a good title, redolent of good autumnal-to-winter food. If you are passing through the valleys of the Lot and Garonne, get some of the famous prunes. I have substituted those plump, stoned, Californian ones.

Le Lapin aux Pruneaux d'Agen
(Rabbit with Prunes)

3½ lbs of rabbit cut into pieces
1 carrot, 1 onion, sliced finely
2 tablespoons of olive oil
1 tablespoons of red wine vinegar
4 oz of fresh belly of pork
2 tablespoons of goose or pork fat
24 button onions
1 tablespoon of plain flour

Half a pint of good stock
1 clove of garlic, chopped
2 carrots, sliced
Bouquet garni, salt and pepper
1 pint of red wine
24 prunes

Soak the prunes overnight in half the red wine and marinate the rabbit pieces in the other half together with the first lot of sliced carrot, onion, vinegar and oil and plenty of freshly ground black pepper.

Next day, cut the pork belly into strips and brown it in the fat in a casserole. Take it out of the fat with a slotted spoon and set aside. Pat the rabbit pieces dry and brown them all over in the fat. Set them aside. Peel and brown the button onions. When they are coloured, sprinkle in the flour, stirring the while until well mixed. Blend in the wine from the prunes and the rabbit, add the stock, garlic, carrots, bouquet garni, season with salt and pepper. Put back the rabbit and pork lardons and bring the pot to a simmer. Cover and leave it to continue simmering very gently for an hour before adding the prunes. Continue cooking for another half hour or until the rabbit is tender when pierced. This is a delicious stew and very good served with a form of French Polenta or Maize Dough.

Maize Dough

Bring 1 pint of water, or milk, 2 oz of goose fat or lard, salt and pepper to taste, to the boil. Sprinkle in 4 oz of maize flour stirring briskly to prevent lumps forming. Reduce the heat and continue stirring for 10-15 minutes until the mixture leaves the sides of the pan. It should be quite firm at this stage. Spread it out on a greased tray or leave in a ball. Allow to cool before slicing. It will seem rather leaden when cold but becomes much lighter when reheated in slices in a lightly oiled frying pan. Or you can grill the slices on one of those grids, thus achieving the black striped look.

30 October 1992

I HAVE JUST spent the weekend at Oare near Pewsey with Walter Baxter and Fergus Provan, owners of the Chanterelle restaurant since its opening (Walter started it then Fergus took it over). I was fed like a fattening calf on my favourite sort of food – gleaming oxtail, wine-dark jugged hare, a soufflé of courgettes rising to the ceiling, all cooked in an Aga. I had never seen a soufflé from an Aga before, it was terrific. I was very interested in a pumpkin soup made by Fergus. All the vegetables are from the garden and he had these great creatures stacked in the garage. The soup was made with chopped pumpkin sautéed with onions, combined in a good stock with the addition of hot chillies, sweet peppers and fresh ginger, simmered until tender, then whizzed in a blender. Very, very good and hot enough to make the eyes water and the hair on your chest grow – ideal for a shooting lunch or survivors from a storm.

They all seemed to be members of Alcoholics Anon round there and I was the only person drinking at a table for five – a curious feeling. Anyhow, to continue the pumpkin theme, as Halloween draws near, I don't like sweetened pumpkin, as in pie, even though it is revered in America. I prefer the use of it in Italy, where it is part of stews, risottos, and stuffed tortelli and is the emblem of the city of Mantua where the best 'zucche gialle' are grown. Here is a good recipe.

Pumpkin Prosciutto Gnocchi

9 oz of puréed pumpkin
1 egg, lightly beaten
1 oz freshly grated parmesan cheese
6 oz of finely chopped prosciutto (or any smoked ham)
6 oz of plain flour
Good scrape of nutmeg – fresh
Salt and pepper

The easiest way to cook the pumpkin is to cut it in half, de-seed it and bake it in a buttered pan, skin side up, for about an hour in a low oven until very tender. Whisk the pumpkin with the egg in a large bowl. Stir in the cheese and prosciutto. Slowly stir in the flour and beat with a wooden spoon until fairly elastic (about four minutes). Add the nutmeg, salt and freshly ground pepper to taste, and beat for another minute. Have a large saucepan of boiling water at the ready. Make little oval shapes with the dough (use two teaspoons if you like). Drop them into the water and, when they rise to the surface, remove them with a slotted spoon and delicately drain on paper towels. Then transfer to a buttered dish of comely aspect. Continue this operation until all the gnocchi dough is used up. Don't put too many gnocchi in the water at the same time, as they need their space. When you are ready to eat, reheat for fifteen minutes in the oven at Gas 3, 350 F, 177 C. Serve with a bowl of fresh parmesan to scatter at will. This is enough for four. A tip from Fergus about potato gnocchi: bake the potatoes don't boil them – makes all the difference to the texture.

Have lots of treats and no tricks I implore you.

27 November 1992

HAPPY 250th Birthday to Wiltons restaurant. It started in 1742 as a shellfish-mongery in Cockspur Street, and has been in Jermyn Street since 1984. I was invited there for what a perfect lunch, nine oysters of sparkling freshness and a partridge – but no bread sauce or crumbs: a bit odd. The people at the next table were generously presented with a pheasant each. I love watching all those immaculate businessmen doing themselves proud over a bird and a bottle even if they are alone.

My other great lunch was to celebrate twenty-five years of Le Gavroche since its original opening in Lower Sloane Street. 'A small but amusing lunch,' it said on the invitation. Amusing it certainly was but I should think we were about sixteen people sitting down. Marvellous food of course: a consommé of gibier with truffles and foie gras, a gratin of cod à la Viennoise, succulent saddle of rabbit with a perfectly executed herb risotto, stuffed baked apple with rum ice cream and an excellent Stilton. Champagne, Madeira with the soup, Courton Charlemagne 1988 with the fish, La Tâche 1981 with the bunny,

Château d'Yquem 1975 with the pudding and Taylor's port 1955 with the

WILTONS RESTAURANT.
WILTON

cheese. What a feast, marred only by a strong smell of mothballs from a man's suit. Albert Roux was our merry host and a good time was had by all. Viva.

After all that you might like to try this:

Venison Dish

Try to find some properly hung if you like the gamey taste, otherwise Sainsbury will do very well if kept in the refrigerator for a few days. You need 2 to 3 medallions of venison for each person. Cut up some streaky unsmoked bacon and fry very gently to extract the fact. Discard the bacon (or eat at will). Toss the medallions in seasoned flour, which you have put in a plastic bag, then fry them in the bacon fat for 5 to 7 minutes, turning frequently. When ready place on a warm dish with a teaspoon of the best bramble jelly on each piece of meat. Keep warm while you make the sauce. Depending on how many you are cooking for add enough really good bouillon to the pan in which you have cooked the venison. Boil briskly to reduce stirring all the juices and fat together. When it looks slightly syrupy mix in a quantity of sour crème fraîche to make a rich sauce. Adjust the seasoning. If you have some fresh blackberries instead of the jelly, cook them lightly in a little red wine and sugar, and spoon onto the medallions.

Serve with fresh egg noodles and tiny brussel sprouts and maybe chestnuts, which are hard work but you can get some very good vacuum-packed ones at grand shops. A side dish of home-made apple sauce is also a delicious addition.

11 December 1992

IT IS NOW exactly two weeks since my motor bicycle was stolen. I think it has been a slow torture form of stealing. First, the straps to hold the basket in place went, then the registration disc was prized off (luckily it only had a few weeks to go). Finally, the whole thing was removed at night by stealth, only to be found a week later, abandoned and damaged in someone's garden in Clapham. So now I am still waiting for the insurer's assessment before my beloved Scootabout can be mended. My life has been ruined, since I am not able to walk far, and I have turned into a sort of hibernating hedgehog rather like Jeff Bernard. The police have been very kind, keeping me informed throughout, though I was rather taken aback to find that they have taken to that PR ploy of calling you by your Christian name ('Hello Jennifer, this is Holly'), never having met you. The policewoman who called me after the discovery of the bike, asked my name and immediately said, 'Right Jennifer, we'll be in touch', very nice of her indeed. So, imitating Noel Coward, I asked if I could call her WPC.

If all this wasn't bad enough, the Income Tax people have been threatening me with bailiff-like treatment if I don't send them money which I already paid a month ago, and Sainsbury's has changed its Scottish Spring Water into something called Caledonian which, if you are not eagle-eyed when purchasing, turns out to have lemon added to it.

On quite a different theme and barging into another's territory, I watched the first instalment on television of *Absolutely Fabulous* and was amazed at all the reviewers' bad notices, including the ones on the wireless of a Saturday evening on Radio 3. I know nothing about the fashion world but I and my elderly uncle thought it terribly funny and roared out loud with laughter. It didn't matter if Miss Saunders was overacting. She is a great knockabout clown, her falls and general dilapidation were worthy of Buster Keaton.

Anyway, I recently found a sumptuous substitute for Christmas pudding in Paul Levy's Christmas book; it is Helge Rubinstein and Sheila Bush's.

Christmas Pudding Ice

(*serves 4-6*)

6 oz of mixed dried and glacé fruits
(currants, raisins, sultanas, orange and citron peel, marrons glacés) all roughly chopped
4 tablespoons of light rum
10 fluid oz of single cream
5 egg yolks
5 oz of caster sugar
2 heaped tablespoons of unsweetened chestnut purée from a tin or a tube
4 oz of chocolate, Menier or similar
10 fluid oz of double cream, whipped thick

Put the fruit to marinate and swell in the rum. Heat the single cream until almost boiling – when the surface trembles a little. Whisk the egg yolks with the sugar in a bowl and pour the near boiling cream over them, whisking constantly. Return the mixture to the saucepan and whisk over a very gentle heat until you have a thick custard. Be very careful, we don't want scrambled eggs. To be safe, use a bain marie, with the pan suspended over, but not touching the simmering water below. When you are happy with the thickness of the custard, whisk in the chestnut purée and then the chocolate broken into small pieces, stir until all is smooth. Add more sugar if you so desire. Leave to cool.

Now incorporate the plumped-up fruits and rum, then fold in the thick whipped cream. Line a pudding basin in foil or fat-safe cling film. Pour in the mixture and freeze. If you can be bothered to give it a stir when it is half frozen, it will improve the texture a bit. Turn it out of the basin at least an hour before serving, letting it 'ripen' in the refrigerator . If the dish is flame-proof, you can warm some rum or brandy in a ladle, light it and pour it over the pudding, which can also have a sprig of holly stuck on the top. A very delicious alternative to the real thing.

Another good thing to have in the refrigerator is a vast bowl of citrus fruit salad. When a guest offers help, sit him down with a very sharp stainless steel knife, a quantity of grapefruits both pink and yellow, oranges and a couple of lemons. Make him peel all the skin and pith off the fruits and cut out each segment over a bowl to secure all the juices. This will take hours and keep everybody happy. Have the fruit salad neat at breakfast or with a good sprinkling of some orange liqueur for a nice sharp desert after one of those far too rich meals.

To use up drying out turkey, cover with tuna mayonnaise overnight and serve as mock vitello tonnato. Garnish with radishes.

Very happy and Holy Christmas to all.

22 January 1993

TERRIBLE HAPPENINGS IN Kingsway. The church of St Anselm and St Cecilia, where my late uncle Canon Bartlett used to be, has done a Windsor Castle and had its roof burned down due to some electrical fault in the organ loft. It will probably take a good year to repair. Poor Father Hugh, the parish priest, was in great distress, unable to minister to his flock over Christmas.

But all is well, the vicar of St George's, Bloomsbury (that beautiful Hawksmoor edifice) has been kindness itself and is going to allow St Anselm's and St Cecilia to box and cox with them. I love that expression. Did you know that it originated with a Mrs Bouncer, a deceitful lodging-house lady, who let the same room to a Mr Cox and Mr Box who, unknown to each other, occupied it alternately, one being out at work all day and the other all night? It's from a farce by J M Morton (1811–1891), adapted from the French. I wonder if Michael Caine knows that...

A good happening was being taken to lunch at the Savoy Grill where I hadn't been for years. It was much cosier than I remembered and the splendid Mr Angelo Maresca, who is in charge, took my helmet as though it were a diadem with much good humour. I had a delicious soup made from sweetcorn with plump oysters floating on the surface, an excellent combination. The dish of the day was boiled gammon and pease pudding, very filling but perfectly presented with beautiful slices of succulent pink meat and a creamy mustard sauce. I was too full for pudding but was eager for the selection of really good British cheeses. Such a treat. The doorman looked after my Honda and found it a good little parking place. Jolly nice place. Who could ask for more?

I was talking to the wandering Giles MacDonogh (he of the historical cooking and wine books) and he stressed the importance of soups in Austria where they play an important role in the structure of meals. Here is a simple, nutritious wine soup, very suitable for these wintry days.

Wachauer Veltlinersuppe

7 oz puff pastry
1 beaten egg
3/4 pint dry white wine
1 1/2 pints good chicken stock

A small stick of cinnamon
1 teaspoon potato starch or cornflour
4 egg yolks
4 tablespoons double cream
Ground cinnamon

Roll out the pastry on a lightly floured board and cut into six triangles. Roll up from the long side to the point, then fashion into crescent shapes. Brush with the beaten egg and chill for thirty minutes. Bake in a pre-heated oven at Gas 6, 400F, 200C, for ten minutes or until risen and golden. Transfer to a wire rack to cool.

Meanwhile, in a good saucepan, bring the wine and stock with the cinnamon stick to the boil, cook until reduced by a third. Remove from the heat, cool slightly and discard the cinnamon stick. Mix the potato starch with the egg yolks and the cream in a large bowl.

Whisk the reduced broth mixture into the egg yolk and cream until thoroughly combined. Return to the saucepan and stir constantly over a gentle heat to thicken but do not let it boil or it will scramble. Pour into warmed bowls and sprinkle with ground cinnamon. Serve with the slightly warmed puff pastry crescents. This serves four.

If you are a sausage fancier, Simply Sausages, at 341 Central Markets, Farringdon Street, London EC1 now has another branch, in Soho at 93 Berwick Street, W1. They have a fantastic array of bangers. Made daily with no artificial horrors and proper natural skins, they are a delight. Do not prick the sausages when cooking, just cook slowly.

If you like you can telephone an order on 0171-287 3482 to collect later. But I should go there once to have a look.

5 February 1993

THE STRANGEST THING to happen to me lately was to be rung up by a nice lady from the BBC. She asked if I had received a script for some programme to do with Chris Kelly, who takes part in the *Food & Wine Show*. I had received no script, but imagined it might be one of those food quizzes in which I have taken part before.

They sent a car to collect me with a lovely driver who asked where I was going. I didn't know either so a lot of telephoning went on and we finally got to the right place, he regaling me throughout with his horror of motor bicycles.

I was led through endless subterranean passages and finally ushered in to a large studio where dear Chris Kelly was rehearsing a lot of real actors. I embraced him tenderly and asked what in heaven's name I was there for. He thrust two pages of some sort of play into my hands and I discovered I was to play a rather tipsy cook (type casting) being questioned by a soppy interviewer. We read it through twice then recorded it and that was that. I can't wait to find out what it was all about – I think it will be on Radio 4 in the spring.

I am fond of anchovies, unlike Craig Brown who seems to have an aversion to them. Grimod de la Reyniere who wrote the *Almanach des Gourmands* was

so devoted to them he seemed to incorporate them into every meal. They have this curious ability to enrich meat without producing a fishy taste, as in this method of roasting lamb.

Roast Leg of Lamb with Anchovy

1 leg of lamb, 3 ½- 4lbs
6 large cloves of garlic
12 anchovy fillets
½ pt vegetable or veal stock
Scant teaspoon of tomato puree
1 teaspoon chopped fresh rosemary
1 tablespoon chopped fresh thyme
Olive oil
Black pepper

Peel the garlic cloves and slice three of them into slithers. Cut about four of the anchovies into little pieces. Insert a bit of each into twenty stab wounds all over the joint. Place in a roasting pan and caress with olive oil. Strew the herbs on top. Place the rest of the anchovy filets in trellis fashion over the meat.

Bake in a preheated oven at Gas Mark 5, 375F, 190C. If you like the flesh pink, cook for fifteen minutes an hour per pound and fifteen minutes more, otherwise cook for twenty minutes per pound, plus another twenty minutes. When cooked, place the meat on its dish and let it rest somewhere warm for fifteen minutes before carving.

Meanwhile blanch the remaining three cloves of garlic in boiling water for three minutes or until just softening. Drain and chop roughly.

When you have removed the meat from the pan, get rid of some of the fat if it abounds, pour in the stock, add the garlic and tomato puree, stir and simmer for as long as it takes to soften the garlic. Press it all through a sieve into a jug, reheat and season with fresh ground pepper. You probably won't need salt, depending on the stock you use.

Carve the joint into thickish wedges and pour the sauce over at will. I serve it with a gratin of thinly sliced carrots and onions (twice as many carrots as onion) fried in butter, moistened with stock, a little scattering of flour and, just before serving, a dash of white wine vinegar and an egg yolk stirred in for thickening, then sprinkled generously with chopped parsley. Some boiled or baked potatoes are all you need with this.

19 February 1993

THE FIRST BIRTHDAY party for *The Oldie* was enormous fun – very like an end-of-term party. We sat at long tables stretching across the room like railway trains, scoffing steak-and-kidney pudding followed by treacle pudding, real schoolboy stuff. Thank heavens we had potted shrimps to start with.

It was a very merry affair with a grand mixture of oldies and youngies. I was opposite Ken Livingstone who seemed a sprightly little fellow full of good humour, demanding tomato ketchup, although he had to rush off in mid-course to 'the House'. He was back in a trice to continue his lunch. (Well done old father Ingrams, may you continue well.)

I have a mystery which perhaps someone could unravel for me. I was sent through the post to my home address a charming and beautifully printed little book by Alan Bennett called *The Lady in the Van*, about an eccentric lady who lived in her van in Mr Bennett's garden. There was a compliments slip with the book and the ominous word 'apologies' written on it. I have no idea who sent it and what the apologies are for. Anyway, they are fully accepted whoever they are from.

The day after *The Oldie* party we entered into the Chinese year of the Cockerel, which symbolises bright and happy days. So let's hope they get it right and a very happy new year to all you cockerels. (I'm a dragon myself.) To celebrate this auspicious happening here is a very good method of making a duck stretch further. It is from the recipe by Deh-Ta Hsiung, wouldn't you know.

Chinese Roast Duck

1 duckling weighing about 4½ lbs
3 tablespoons of dark soy sauce

Stuffing

4 oz glutinous or round pudding rice
5 medium Chinese dried mushrooms
1 oz dried shrimps
The giblets of the duckling
2 oz bamboo shoots

2 oz cooked ham
2 tablespoons of oil
2 spring onions, finely chopped
1 ½ tablespoons of light soy sauce
1 ½ tablespoons of rice wine or dry sherry
A pinch of monosodium glutamate
Salt to taste

Brush the duck skin with the dark soy sauce. Soak the rice in 6fl oz of boiling water for 20-25 minutes. Soak the dried mushrooms in warm water for 30 minutes. Squeeze dry, discard the stalks and cut into pea-size cubes. Soak the shrimps in warm water for 20 minutes, rinse and drain. Boil the duck's gizzard in water, simmering for 15 minutes. Remove the flesh and dice with the heart, liver, bamboo shoots and ham. Heat the oil in a wok or large frying-pan and stir-fry the mushrooms, shrimps, giblets, bamboo shoots, ham and spring onions for 1 minute. Mix in the light soy sauce and wine, the rice and its soaking water, monosodium glutamate and salt to taste. Bring all this to the boil, reduce heat and cook for 8-10 minutes until all the liquid is absorbed.

Pack this stuffing into the duck cavity and close up the tail opening. Stitch it or secure with toothpicks. Place the duck on a wire rack in a roasting tin and cook in a preheated oven at Gas 6, 400F, 200C, for 30 minutes, then lower the heat to Gas 4, 350F, 180C, for a further 45 minutes.

To serve, spread the stuffing out on a suitable dish, chop the duck into bite-sized pieces and arrange temptingly on top of the stuffing.

If you find some of the ingredients difficult to obtain, don't worry. It will be delicious whatever you do, I'm sure.

5 March 1993

READING ABOUT THE 'Return of the Puddings from Hell' (*Oldie* 26) I remember Dead Baby well, a terrible grey-white slug of a pudding. But at our convent we had a rather good jam roly-poly known as Reverend Mother's Arm, as the lady in question had a false one with a beautifully modelled hand at the end, always neatly gloved. She used to stick pins into it to our great fascination and delight. A fierce and upright creature who had the misfortune of being unable to pronounce her 'Rs', she was named Reverend Mother Rita of the Resurrection which of course created cruel and merry laughter all round. She expelled me at the age of fifteen, but as I had been there since I was seven I reckon I won.

My beloved greengrocers, Fred and Caroline Foster of the Tatchbrook Street market, had their baby daughter christened this Sunday – Frederica Amelia. I had been invited, but due to an absolutely stinking cold felt it unwise and unkind to go. I do wish I could have attended, it sounded absolutely marvellous. Father Russell of the Holy Apostles performed the sacrament, then they all went off for oysters and vintage champagne to the Boisdale Restaurant in Eccleston Street. That's what I call a very good christening.

I suppose it will be Lent when you read this, Ash Wednesday past and gone. As we have no carnival here, and as only two days of fasting are required there seems very little hardship left, though most people give up something, or better still, do something elevating. The fasting laws were made long ago and have never been updated, so that they now amount to what most people eat normally: one full but meatless meal plus two little snacky ones. Good Friday has always meant scrummy fish pie to me, Shrove Tuesday has its pancakes and in France Ash Wednesday has its soup with glorious pistou. From Elisabeth Luard's *European Festival Food* which is very much to my liking, I recommend:

Ash Wednesday Bean Soup with Pistou

(*serves 4*)

The Soup

6 oz white haricot beans, soaked overnight
2 large carrots, scraped and chunked
2 small turnips, peeled and chunked

3 sticks of celery, washed and chopped
A bouquet garni of bayleaf, parsley and thyme
2 pints of water
1 large potato, peeled and cubed
Quarter of a cabbage, shredded
2 leeks, washed and cut into fine rings
Salt and pepper

The Pistou

4 large cloves of garlic (one each) roughly chopped
1 cup basil leaves minus their stalks
1 slice of stale but good bread
Quarter of a pint of olive oil
Salt

Drain the soaked beans and rinse them. Put them in a soup-pot with the carrots, turnips, celery and bouquet garni. Add the water but no salt yet. Bring to the boil, turn down the heat to simmering point, cover and leave to cook gently for one and a half hours until the beans are soft. After an hour add the potato.

Meanwhile, make the pistou. Put all the ingredients into the liquidiser, or pound up the first three ingredients in a mortar and add the oil gradually.

Just before you are ready to serve the soup, take out the bouquet garni and stir in the cabbage and the leeks. Add salt and fresh ground pepper to your taste, bring back to the boil and serve.

Let everyone stir in their own pistou. 'Heaven is a Lenten bean soup. Plenty more tomorrow and tomorrow.'

I usually make twice the amount given. Why not?

If you have given up drink for Lent and get a bit bored with soda water and lemon, try no-calorie American Ginger Ale with a drop or two of Angostura bitters. I find this quite grown-up.

19 March 1993

I WENT TO a very good funeral last week in Bath and was amazed at the size of the Catholic church, St John's on South Parade, which is not far from the Abbey. It is a fine building with a very jolly painted ceiling, but I had no time to discover its history. We all trooped back to the splendid widow's house and had a wonderful wake ably attended to by charming girls in red waistcoats overseen by a young but expert chef in the kitchen. Lots of champagne with delicious, hot eaty-firsties followed by a full blown lunch. I love a good funeral when there is no tragedy present. Unlike a wedding you know most of the people and they are usually better dressed in their mourning weeds.

I remained in the country for the weekend at Sutton Veney where my host Milo Parmoor was having fun with his latest toy. He had bought in Germany the most enormous garden umbrella, the size of a normal room, which rose from the centre of the terrace like the Dome of Discovery of yesteryear. A huge step ladder had just been delivered that was necessary for the removing of the cover. It took three people to get this giant parasol up and spread out, but it did look marvellous and will give plenty of shade to enable people to eat outside on those two hot days in the year if it isn't blown away by a gale.

One of the hazards of going away is other people's beds. I spent the nights in a Thurber-like frenzy fighting with a duvet. I can't manage them and end up totally exhausted. Apart from that I had a lovely time, ending with a lunch for 12 on Sunday after a disastrous guitar-accompanied Mass in Warminster with the 'kiddies' swarming all over the altar.

My other treat was to attend the seventieth birthday of Charley, the Earl of Carlisle at Boodles club, a very swelegant and delightful dinner party in a beautiful room. Very good food but not a birthday cake in sight. (However I led a chorus of 'Happy Birthday', so honour was satisfied.) The other night I went to Harvey's restaurant to see Marco Pierre White receive some honour from France. It was also the inauguration of a very grand new publication called *Gastronomica International* which will come out four times a year for the princely sum of £53.95. This edition contains divine receipts from Karl Wannemacher in Berlin, our own Marco Pierre White and Yves Thuriès from Cordes in France. Marco threw out the odd journalist and a good time was had by all, including a fully robed mayor.

I am very fond of that tragic looking fish, the gurnard. It has firm, sweet flesh and is still inexpensive. Elisabeth Luard has produced another excellent and informative book, *A Taste of the Country*, where I found this tasty little dish.

Gurnard with Orange Butter

4-5lbs golden gurnard
The zest and juice of 1 small orange
4 oz butter, softened
2 tablespoons of chopped fresh
tarragon (or 1 of freeze dried)
Salt and fresh ground pepper
Aromatic oil

Clean, wipe and skin the fish or get your fishmonger to do so. Trim off the tail.

Beat the orange juice into the butter then add the grated zest and the tarragon. Keep in the refrigerator until needed.

Season the skinned fish and rub lightly with aromatic oil. Wrap in cooking foil and bake in a pre-heated oven at 190C, 375F, Gas 5, for 25 minutes. Check to see if it's cooked through by lifting the flesh at the backbone. When it comes away easily you know it is ready. Serve with a knob of orange butter on top to melt into the succulent flesh.

To make aromatic oil, immerse a sprig of your herb in a bottle of extra virgin olive oil and leave to infuse for a week or two. The infused oil should be kept in the refrigerator and used up within a month.

28 May 1993

I WENT ON an extraordinary outing to the theatre, by bus from Boodle's club in St James's Street to the Albery in St Martin's Lane, to see *Hay Fever* before it finally closed. Quite the most comfortable way of theatre going. We all gathered at the club's bar for drinks and dainty sandwiches, a marvellous sight to behold, all these well dressed men in their perfectly cut suits with their doughty wives beside them bristling with fresh hair settings and sensible frocks. On the right dot we clambered into the waiting charabanc, were whisked off to the play, which was hilarious as usual, with that girl who does the Philadelphia cheese advertisements stealing the show again, and then the real bliss of not having to find a taxi or a parking ticket on your car – there was our faithful bus waiting to return the jolly party back to Boodle's for an excellent supper. Such a good idea.

I finally made it to the impenetrable Quaglino's by dint of an invitation from Tesco to sample their 'Ultimate Tomato', the Flavourtop. This has taken four years of research to produce, we were informed. After three seriously deep speeches we were given a glass of water, a water biscuit to clear the palate and some chunks of this awesome tomato to eat. Well, they were certainly deep red, shiny and healthy skinned as proclaimed but the taste was very ordinary, same as your usual run of the mill tomato, nothing to compare with those gnarled, aromatic, heavenly tasting ones from Italy or Greece, or even a humble home-grown one from the garden. I see that Safeway is also plugging their new tomato range under the 'FlavourGrown' label as well as importing from Provence and Spain, so it is obviously a fight to the finish for the tomato of the month. I reckon you need a good seed and plenty of sun and a little less of the in-depth research to get a good taste, but it will be interesting to compare the various offerings as the summer arrives.

I have been sent a delightful little first issue of *Convivium, The Journal of Good Eating*. It will be available by subscription at £25 per year, or single copies can be bought from Books for Cooks, 4 Blenheim Crescent, London W11. This first issue is dedicated to the memory of Elizabeth David and contains personal memoirs by some of her close friends. Lovely little book, I wish it well.

Let us have a truly seasonal dish from Harry's Bar.

Marinated Salmon with Asparagus

For the marinade:

4 fl oz of dry white wine
8 fl oz of fresh lemon juice
4 teaspoons of caster sugar
5 oz of malden salt
12 peppercorns
1 clove of garlic, crushed
3 rosemary sprigs, 3 thyme sprigs, 1 bay leaf

2 lbs of salmon fillet in one piece
30 asparagus spears

Combine all the marinade ingredients in a shallow bowl large enough to hold the salmon. Mix well until salt and sugar have dissolved. Put the salmon skin-side up in the marinade, cover well with plastic wrap and refrigerate for 48 hours, turning it once every 12 hours. Drain the salmon and discard the marinade. Gently scrape the whitened flesh from the surface of the fish then return it to the refrigerator. Clean and steam the asparagus until just tender then rinse under cold water. Drain on a dish cloth. When cool, dress with a vinaigrette made from three tablespoons of red wine vinegar, quarter of a teaspoon of dry mustard, salt and fresh ground pepper to taste and 8 fl oz of best olive oil whisked in until emulsified. Using a very sharp knife and holding it almost parallel to the work surface, slice the salmon paper-thin. Arrange the asparagus on six plates and cover them completely with slices of salmon. Sprinkle each serving with a little extra-virgin olive oil (Laudemio I Bonsi is perfect for this). Serve with some dry toast and drink Plinius-Mastroberardino.

As an alternative to asparagus you can use fennel, cooked and chopped then dressed as above but minus the vinegar.

11 June 1993

I HAVEN'T BEEN up to much since my visit to Cambridge just before the communist Bank Holiday. I was on a wireless quiz about food and had a sublime dinner at the 'Midsummer House' restaurant on the river. The best fresh foie gras, grilled then placed on a cunning sauce of roast Bramley apple and cassis, absolutely stunning and as good as I have ever had, followed by a triumphant aiguillette of beef (strips of the tenderest top rump, larded, marinated and cooked with red wine, brandy and onions, served very rare) arranged on a pile of garlic mashed potatoes. Yummo. Then yesterday I had the perfect spring lunch. Where? Here, at *The Oldie*, by courtesy of Christopher Bowerbank, the lookalike of young Beethoven, architect and landlord. Jubby Ford, our beloved editor's ravishing daughter, produced a succulent pink rack of lamb with tiny new potatoes, tiny green beans and a really good salad of numerous green leaves, with a real taste and dressed with art and simplicity. Another big yummo. Willie Rushton was there in usual splendid form. He does the most extraordinary imitation of the tuba from somewhere within his cheeks. What a jolly lunch.

My only other excitement was a performance of Handel's *Ariodante* at the Coliseum where they had appeared to use the contents of a dressing-up box to clothe the characters. Ginevra, the tragic heroine, appeared in a white tulle strapless evening dress, as if she were off to Queen Charlotte's Ball, and the King of Scotland was done up like a cardinal. However, the music was beautiful, and it was an interesting experience, even though I scarpered after the second act.

I was looking at one of those *Food Lover's Introduction to Britain*, which are a very good idea for travelling folk or tourists, and found a good rabbit dish from East Anglia. I love rabbit – I trust you do too.

Rabbit Casserole with Dumplings

1 wild rabbit, jointed
6 oz unsmoked streaky bacon
2 large onions, sliced
8 oz of sliced carrots
8 oz of button or sliced mushrooms
1 apple, peeled, cored and diced

Bouquet garni of bay, rosemary, thyme amd parsley
2 tablespoons of plain flour
Quarter of a pint dry vermouth, white wine or cider
Three quarters of a pint good chicken or veal stock

Heat the oven to Gas mark 3, 325F, 170C. Chop the bacon into small bits, leaving the rind on for flavour. Fry gently in a casserole with a little oil until the fat exudes. Add the rabbit pieces and brown all over. Stir in the onions to brown a little then add the carrots, mushrooms, apple and bouquet garni. Sprinkle the flour over the top then stir in to the rabbit mixture to coat evenly. Cook for about a minute, stirring the while, then pour in the wine and stock. Mix well, season with salt and freshly ground black pepper, and bake in the oven for one and a half hours. Meanwhile, make the dumplings. Mix together 3oz self-raising flour, half an ounce shredded beef suet, one tablespoon of chopped parsley and/or chives, the grated peel from about half a lemon, and salt and pepper. Add enough water to make a soft dough. Divide into 12 pieces and roll into little balls. When the rabbit has cooked for over an hour, place the dumplings within, on top of the contents, cover and continue the cooking until the rabbit is tender and the dumplings are cooked through. Makes enough for four.

An easy pudding from Scotland's Murdo MacSween:

Caledonian Cream

Half a pint of double cream
1 tablespoon of orange marmalade of your choice
1 tablespoon of lemon juice
2oz caster sugar
2 tablespoons of The Glenlivet whisky

Whip the cream until thick. Combine all the other ingredients then gently fold in the cream. Spoon into dainty pots. This is enough for two. Awfully good.

9 July 1993

APROPOS OF NOTHING, how often do you get asked a really funny question? The other day Willie Landels (late of *Harpers & Queen*), who was brought up in Italy, which has produced a weird type of accent to his speaking voice, telephoned me with this curious query: 'Gennyfare,' – this is Willie-speak – 'fwat isdat gayme they play in Scotland, fwhen they pick up a telegraph pole and throw it in the air?'

I have managed at last to sample the food in Quaglinos, as I was kindly taken to lunch there. Let me tell you it was no pleasure at all. I ordered sweetbreads *en croute* to start with, which I love. They arrived so overcooked and so overcrumbed as to be unrecognisable, and were served with a sauce of such strength it could have masked a buffalo's hide. The croute was a round of pastry sitting on the side. I followed this with rabbit cooked with prosciutto, which was dry as old blotting paper and wildly oversalted. Dear oh dear. Perhaps I was just unlucky. I do hope so, as it is a jolly place with charming creatures serving you – but no untipped cigarettes in the cigarette-girl's tray.

During the mini-heatwave I fled from our top-floor flat which becomes a fiery furnace in such weather and took refuge with Patrick Procktor, the long, thin artist. His entire drawing-room is filled with an enormous canvas on which he is painting a huge volcano – but apart from that, his house is wonderfully cool and has a basement leading out on to a tiny tree-shaded terrace where we had an exquisite little picnic. He produced iced white wine, red salmon caviar and sour cream, and I had brought a perfect melon and an avocado from the market, together with Parma ham and bread from my lovely Italian shop in Tatchbrook Street. Cheese and a bowl of olives completed our delight.

Sainsbury's is now selling large, plump chicken wings which, after the thighs, are my favourite parts of the bird, being on the bone and juicier than the breast. They make very good picnic food. You get eight in a pack and I marinate them for about two hours. Rub crushed garlic into them, and lie in a flame-proof dish, sprinkled with thyme and a crushed bay leaf, salt, freshly ground pepper, olive oil and lemon juice. Turn them every now and then. When ready to cook, add some good jellied chicken stock to cover the bottom of the pan. Pre-heat the oven to Gas 5, 375F, 190C and cook for about 30 minutes until tender and succulent.

Alternatively, you could grill or barbecue them. To produce a Chinesey taste, dowse the wings with soy sauce and add Chinese five spice to the marinade – and a little grated ginger doesn't come amiss. Just before cooking insert some strips of spring onion.

Broad bean time is nearing, so I shall remind you of an old receipt of mine.

Broad Beans Fitz

Make a dressing with quarter of a pint of best olive oil, lemon juice, salt and fresh ground pepper to suit your taste. Cut six rashers of bacon into bits and fry or grill until crisp. Drain on paper towels. Put one and a half pounds of shelled broad beans into boiling salted water, cook until just tender. Drain through a colander then refresh under cold water.

Have four hard-boiled eggs at the ready. Chop roughly and mix with a good amount of chopped parsley and chives. Place the beans (patted dry) in a pretty china dish and sprinkle with the crisp bacon pieces. Pile the eggs and herbs on top, then form a lattice of anchovies (a tin and a half) over all. Chill slightly and just before serving pour the dressing over the lot. This makes an excellent first course served with good crusty bread or toast.

Delicious hint from Hugo Arnold in the *Evening Standard*: add one dessert spoon of balsamic vinegar to 1lb of sliced strawberries, marinate for an hour. Wonderful.

23 July 1993

HORRORS! HERE I am sitting on a perfect summer's day and I have just received an invitation from Debenhams to attend 'Christmas, A Family Occasion', in July. I'm sure it will be lovely but with Midsummer's Day already over it is rather a depressing thought. I also had a letter from some organisation opposed to the eating of *foie gras*, comparing the feeding methods of the goose with making them smoke continual cigarettes and then selling their lungs as a delicacy. Well, I don't think you could force a goose to smoke. They don't even like cigarettes and they do love corn and even if they did smoke I am sure the lungs would be disgusting. So it is a typically foolish argument. Why are these protesters so stupid?

I have just spent a splendid long weekend in a miraculously fine-weathered Cumberland. (It usually cats and dogs for me up there.) The occasion was the sixty-fifth birthday of my dear friend Patricius Senhouse, he of the 'Broad Beans Fitz' recipe in the last issue. A great party was held at lunch time on Sunday, catered for by charming girls in black and white with sweet faces, perfect manners and great expertise. Those marvellous little Morecambe Bay shrimps piled on to biscuits were served with the drinks. How good they are and how difficult to find! And now they are being threatened by the ghastly EEC who do not approve of the families of Morecambe Bay dealing and peeling them in their own back yards as they have done for years. Bad cess to them and all bureaucrats. Our main course was a delightful chicken dish with a lemon and watercress sauce, buttery little new potatoes and mange-tout, summery, light and quite delicious, followed by a killer chocolate cake steeped in brandy and served with great ladles of clotted cream. Oh ho, what a feast. I am always so impressed by parties in the country, everyone is so punctual and as if by some magic signal they all leave at some suitable time – very unlike our haphazard London Sunday lunches where people leave at nine in the evening saying they are so sorry to break up the party.

We returned to the Smoke on Monday after another sumptuous lunch at Newton Reigny with Mary and Ian Lowe. A mimosa of their own bantam eggs, a sea trout with not only mayonnaise but also an exquisite sauce made by blending an avocado pear with crème fraîche, salt and pepper and a touch of sherry vinegar – we must all try it at once. A fine strawberry sorbet followed and some magnificent cheeses just brought over from France. The Livarot was a dream. These Lowes breed whippets and there seemed to be hundreds of them surrounding us in the garden, beautifully behaved, reclining in graceful positions, it was like being in a beautiful French tapestry. We picked up a lovely Lord called Northbourne, I think – a great asset as we had a puncture and he helped fix it in a trice. So we returned home thoroughly contented.

I was invited to the German Embassy by CMA (food and drink from Germany) for 'Specialities in Summertime', all stunningly arranged. But I don't really like German food. The sausages and smoked pork loins all seem to be made of rubber and the sweet things, including the yoghurts and cheesecakes, taste of cinnamon or strong vanilla. The cheeses are bland but the beer is very good if you like beer, and there are some good packeted sauces like

Hollandaise. The Reichenhaller Alpine Salt has a very good taste and the Jensens Pâtés in little tins are excellent.

Try this:

Summery Yoghurt and Cucumber Soup

Grate a peeled and seeded cucumber coarsely. Sprinkle with two teaspoons of Alpine salt. Leave in a colander for 30 minutes. Rinse and drain. In a large bowl mix 28oz of plain yoghurt, two crushed cloves of garlic, two teaspoons of white wine vinegar, two tablespoons of fresh chopped dill, one tablespoon of fresh chopped mint and a quantity of fresh ground pepper to suit your taste. Stir in the grated cucumber. If you think the mixture is too thick you can add a little cold vegetable stock but not too much. Cover and chill for at least two hours. When about to serve adjust the seasoning, sprinkle with dill and dish out. Refreshing.

6 August 1993

MY HIGHLIGHT OF the past fortnight was a magnificent picnic given by Sarah Toynbee Towler, William Joll and Richard Barrowclough on the occasion of the two men's fortieth birthdays. We had to get to Queen's Eyot, an island in the Thames near Windsor where the little darlings from Eton row – an enchanted place with a pavilion at one end then a great stretch of greensward surrounded by trees. All we had to do was bring a rug and a bottle of champagne. A first class barbecue was smoking away, expertly handled for once. Mr O'Hagan's super sausages from Greenwich were cooked to a turn, as were the chicken satays. Ciabatta bread split in half, stuffed with omelettes and aubergines and then squished, made a terrific type of sandwich. There were great salads in enormous bowls, the best of cheeses, summer fruits, and packets of crisps for the children, of course. It all made for an exemplary Fête Champêtre. I had made five large roast meat loaves and a beautiful girl had made a very good tomato sauce to go with them. There must have been well over a hundred people there. It was a wonderful sight to see all the rakes of yesteryear now married to ravishing girls and proudly clutching their latest babies to their manly bosoms. And we didn't lose one child – a miracle with the river so handy. Joy reigned supreme. It was a lovely day.

The *Spectator* summer party was even more crowded than usual (if that is possible) and great fun. I met Lady Thatcher who must have been astonished at the crush, which she braved manfully. Like actors seen on the screen she appeared much smaller than I had imagined, with beautiful skin.

I have had two excellent restaurant meals for a nice change. The first was at Claridges, where I hadn't been for years. I was invited by one of those fantastic American women, well over eighty, who has done everything and known everyone. She now lives in a 16th-century house of great splendour in Cuernavaca, Mexico, having left her villa in Vicenza named after her (the Villa Lambert). Claridges produced an exquisite duck salad with artichokes and a perfect piece of cod. I must say it is very nice there, so cool and airy, with great service. The other treat was dinner at Daphne's in Draycott Avenue, where I consumed a dream of a soup, bruschetta, which contained clams and mussels swimming in a saffron-flavoured creamy broth accompanied by garlic grilled toast, followed by a confit of duck with haricot beans, all sticky with crisp skin. Couldn't have been better.

I shall give you the receipt for my offering to the picnic.

Roast Meat Loaf

1lb best sausage meat
1lb each of minced beef, pork and turkey
Half a pound chicken or turkey livers
Half a pound unsmoked streaky bacon
Half a pound mushrooms
1 large onion grated
10 juniper berries, crushed
Three fat cloves of garlic, crushed
Nutmeg, powdered allspice, rosemary, thyme & bay leaf
Salt and pepper
1 egg

Slice the mushrooms and sauté in butter, sprinkle with nutmeg and leave to cool. Slice the livers. In a large bowl, place all the minced meats, the livers, the sausage meat, the grated onion, crushed garlic and juniper berries and a good teaspoon each of allspice and thyme. Season with salt and about 20 turns of the pepper mill. Break the egg into the bowl and mix everything together most thoroughly. Hands are best for this operation. Oil an oven tin. Place the mixture in the tin and mould into an oval mound. Adorn with the strips of bacon, criss-crossed Union Jack-wise tucking the ends under the loaf. Put a couple of bay leaves on top and sprinkle with rosemary needles. Place in a pre-heated oven Gas Mark 8, 450F, 230C, for quarter of an hour then lower the heat to Gas Mark 4, 350F, 180C, and cook for a further hour and a half. When cooked there will be an abundance of juices at the bottom of the pan. Save them for another day's flavouring to a soup or egg dish. Remove the loaf, place on a platter and serve with tomato sauce. Hot or cold as you prefer.

20 August 1993

I GET SOME strange things through the post. A nice farmer sent me some steak to show how good his meat was, but unfortunately it hit the middle of a postal strike and lay festering in some unknown post sack. When it was finally delivered it was like opening a grave, the stench was appalling and the contents even more terrible to behold though, thank God, the meat was secured in a plastic pack. We buried it in the garden at dead of night. (I should have put it in a pot of basil.) However, it was a kind thought and was probably delicious before the post got at it.

This week's offering is quite a different matter. I cannot imagine why Crosse & Blackwell should send me various packets of 'Simply Fix' dehydrated foods. They are the sort of lazy approach to cooking which I abominate, containing unspeakable things like flavour enhancers, monosodium glutamate, and vinegar solids – yuk. I tried the Pasta Carbonara out of duty. 'Ready in less than seven minutes, this tasty product can be eaten either as a snack or as part of a main meal' runs the blurb. (Whoever heard of spaghetti alla carbonara being used as 'part' of a meal?) 'Just add water and milk and butter for a quick cook.' I followed the instructions to the second and produced a fine saucepan of paper-hanging paste with that well known off-cheesey aroma. If you want that delicious, classical dish this is how you make it, not very difficult. This amount is enough for six but you can reduce the quantities for less.

Spaghetti alla Carbonara

One and a half pounds of spaghetti or fedelini (De Cecco is best)
1 tablespoon of olive oil
6 oz of pancetta or streaky bacon cut into strips
6 eggs
2 tablespoons of cream
Salt and freshly ground pepper
Quarter of a pound of freshly grated parmesan or pecorino cheese

Make the sauce while the spaghetti is cooking in lots of salted boiling water. Put the oil and strips of bacon in a large saucepan (large enough to take the spaghetti when ready). Cook gently until the fat of the bacon is completely transparent. Remove and drain the spaghetti when it is still very much *al dente* and put it into the pan with the bacon. Leave them there until they are completely cooked. Meanwhile beat the eggs with the cream, add a little salt and a good amount of ground black pepper. At the last moment, when the spaghetti is just right, pour in the cream mixture, stir and mix rapidly, transfer to a warmed serving bowl and eat immediately accompanied by the grated cheese. A dish fit for a king. Begone foul packets. 'They out-Herod Herod, pray you avoid them'.

From the false to the natural. I also received five tiny little pots of honey from the Honey Bureau. Australian Eucalyptus, Tasmanian Leatherwood, Orange Blossom, Greek Pine and Chinese Acacia – the last of which I shall use for Peking Duck this evening. They all have distinct flavours of their own, the Greek one being the darkest with a little hint of Retsina about it. They can be found in most major supermarkets and – dread word – health shops. I like the idea of this Honey, Yogurt Brulee. Serves four.

Honey, Yogurt Brulee

Half a pint of crème fraîche or whipped double cream
Half a pint of thick set natural yogurt (Total Greek is best)
3 tablespoons of clear honey
2 tablespoons of soft brown sugar
A few flaked almonds

Mix together the crème fraîche or whipped cream with the yogurt. Pour into a fireproof dish and swirl the honey over the top. Sprinkle the soft brown sugar evenly over the surface, then scatter the almonds all over. Chill for an hour or so. Pre-heat your grill for about five minutes, place the dish: under the grill until the top is brown and bubbling. Serve at once – but don't burn your lips.

17 September 1993

I HAVE BEEN learning about gin. It is far more complex than I had imagined. Gin is treated with great reverence by its distillers, in the same way as the great malt whisky producers revere their secret methods. I visited the Beefeater distillery, just behind the Oval cricket ground, where from the top floor you can watch play to your heart's content. The reception room has very curious chairs, with only one arm-rest, which gives a feeling of drunkenness to start you off with.

I hadn't realised that some naughty gin makers have been lowering their alcohol volume to 37.5 per cent from the usual 40 per cent while still charging the same price to the public. Not so Beefeaters, whose gin is the only premium Distilled London dry gin which is actually distilled in London. They retain their 40 per cent alcohol volume to ensure the taste remains the same – and it does. We tasted the stronger and the weaker samples, and the difference was quite startling from the point of scent and palate. But I suppose mixed with tonic it wouldn't really matter.

The flavourings for this gin are deeply exotic. Called 'botanicals', they are gathered from all over the world – juniper berries from Italy, citrus peels and almonds from Spain, coriander from Russia and Eastern Europe and angelica from the fields of Flanders are joined by other 'secret ingredients' known only to the distiller, the charming Mr Brian Martin, who has been distilling there for 34 years and will only give up his secret on his deathbed, I like to think. He drinks his simply with water and has a beautiful complexion, so he must be getting it right.

This gin is made with pure grain spirit (wheat) then distilled by vapourising through all the botanicals to get the flavour. It's as simple as that. But the days of 'Drunk for a penny, dead drunk for two pence' have gone long since 1750, when the availability and low cost of gin was denounced as the major cause of crime in London.

I use gin whenever I am cooking pork chops or a roast, as the juniper flavour is excellent with this meat. Add about 2 fl oz to your marinade of lemon and olive oil for the chops, or pour the same amount over a roast half way through the cooking to mingle with the juices and form part of the subsequent gravy. It's also good with some vermouth (as for a cocktail) in the marinade for a rich beef stew.

Try this fake stroganoff made with pork fillet instead of beef, adapted from Prue Leith's little book *Quick and Easy*.

Pork Stroganoff

1¾ lbs pork fillet
1 tablespoon olive oil
1 oz butter
2 onions thinly sliced
2 tablespoons of gin
9 fl oz soured cream
Salt, pepper and paprika

Remove any fat from the pork and cut across the grain into 1½-inch strips. Heat half the oil and butter in a large frying pan, cook the onions gently until golden brown. Transfer to a plate. Increase the heat, add more butter and oil and fry half the pork quickly for three minutes until lightly brown. Transfer to a plate and cook remaining pork in the same way. Return all the meat to the pan, pour the gin over the top and heat gently for two minutes, set light to it and when the flame dies add the onions, soured cream, and salt and fresh ground pepper. Bring to the boil, sprinkle with chopped parsley and a goodly

pinch of paprika and serve immediately with some plain boiled basmati rice or buttered noodles. A salad of green beans flavoured with lemon and garlic is a perfect accompaniment.

Sliced button mushrooms can be added – fry them after the onions and transfer to the plate before cooking the meat.

1 October 1993

PHEASANT SHOOTING BEGINS on October 1st – not such an exciting event as it used to be, as they are now reared in such quantities as to be practically tame and can hardly get off the ground, so plump and fat are they after having been reared on good corn before being released into the wild. This corn also produces that nasty yellow fat they now abound with. I try to remove as much as possible. The good side of all this rearing is of course that they are really quite cheap now, not much more than a good chicken.

Unfortunately the plucked birds in the markets have usually not been hung long enough. An unhung pheasant really has no more flavour than a chicken and is a good deal drier. I reckon on at least nine days hanging, so it is better to get plucked ones and hang them yourself. But there's the rub. The plucking gets very expensive and is often very badly executed. A first-class poulterer will deliver the goods in perfect condition, but it is a good idea to learn to pluck your own – it is not difficult and gives a great sense of achievement.

There is a good, large paperback out, published by the *Shooting Times – The Art of Game Cookery* by Rosemary Wadey – which would be useful to new game cooks. She cooks the small birds too long for my taste, 30-45 minutes. I would give it 25 but that is a matter of personal choice, only to be discovered by experience. However, she has some good pâtés and terrines. This is a coarse pâté which I prefer.

Pheasant and Liver Pâté

Half a raw, high pheasant
12 oz of pig's liver
12 oz of streaky bacon rashers, derinded
1 large onion peeled
2 cloves of garlic crushed
1 egg beaten
3-4 tablespoons of brandy or port
Salt and black pepper
2 bay leaves

Strip the meat from the bone and mince or process fairly finely with the liver, half the bacon and the onion. Add the garlic, egg, brandy or port and plenty of fresh ground black pepper and salt to taste. Stretch the remaining bacon rashers and use to line a well buttered 2lb loaf tin with the bay leaves in the base of it. Spoon the pâté mixture into the tin, folding over the ends of the bacon to partly cover it. Stand the tin in a roasting pan containing about one and a half inches of water and cook in a pre-heated oven at Gas 4, 180C, 350F, for about one and a half hours, when you see the pâté coming away from the sides of the tin. Remove the tin from the water, cool a little, then cover with greaseproof paper and a weight. Cool, then refrigerate for several hours. Turn out and serve in slices with hot toast or French bread. I think I would use a whole bird and make double the quantity. The second one could be frozen for a future occasion.

15 October 1993

I HAVE AT last had a sebaceous cyst removed from the back of my neck, a hard thing like a marble. I had it out in 1989 but due to inefficiency it returned. My present doctor wrote to the new Westminster and Chelsea hospital in January or February; I duly got an appointment on the 19th April only to be told I must go to another doctor in surgery. A letter was then dictated stating I had already waited over three months so hurry it up please. In July, no appointment having been made, I telephoned the original doctor and got the secretary, who said she would check and telephone me back if all was not well. She didn't call. Two weeks later I insisted on talking to the doctor himself. Lo and behold his letter had not got through the computers. Then, fired by guilt (I hope) they asked if I could come in immediately which of course I couldn't. So I went the next week to be looked at and three weeks later they finally took it out with much blood letting and the wrong instruments, as the right ones were not available. Thank you very much Mrs Bottomley. Did you know they spent £125,000 on the plants alone at this ridiculous place and heaven knows what they paid for the tropical fish (which die daily, so one of the staff told me). Holy cow, no wonder the NHS is in such a mess.

I just wanted to get that off my chest. Now to happier things. I did rather well last week after two sessions of being quizzed and photographed for a magazine. I was twice taken out to lunch to Simply Nico in Rochester Row. I love this restaurant, I love the staff who are young and cheerful and expert – such a relief and the food is always perfectly delicious with the sort of brasserie things I like: little hot chicken-liver mousses, dark, shiny oxtail, really tender kidneys and, of course, their most famous chips which are top. (Rifkind was there with his tie flung over his shoulder in a curious way, perhaps to keep it out of the splendid saffron fish soup.)

I was wandering through our market last Thursday and spied something really exciting on the fishmonger's stall, a whole salmon roe, which I bought for £2. I had never seen one on sale before but I love the red caviar which used to be available in jars (not lumpfish). I didn't really know what to do with it, but having seen the Russians on TV preparing the real caviar I tried to emulate them. Removing the membrane is quite tricky, taking time and patience. I then flavoured the eggs with salt, pepper, lemon juice and a dash of vodka and served it with some grated hard-boiled eggs, fromage frais and spring onions. But it was too bland. What it needed was much more salt than you would imagine. I added this and packed the lot into a jar to chill overnight. It did the trick and the eggs tasted superb. But I would be grateful if anyone knows the right way to deal with this beautiful titbit.

If you have made a chocolate cake or torte here is a sumptuous chocolate cream glaze from Mark Eastment. It would also do very well to pour over ice cream.

Chocolate Cream Glaze

9 oz of best bittersweet chocolate
8 oz of double cream
Half a fluid oz of cognac (optional)

Heat the cream to boiling point and pour three quarters of it over the broken pieces of chocolate in a bowl. Cover for five minutes to allow the chocolate to melt. Add the rest of the cream and gently stir together until smooth, trying not to create air bubbles. Pass through a fine strainer, stir in the optional cognac and allow to cool until just tepid. Then pour over the cake, torte or ice cream – even poached pears or peaches if you so desire.

Jeanne Strang's excellent book *Goose Fat and Garlic* is out in paperback (Kyle Cathie). Buy it if you can. Really good.

29 October 1993

I HAVE JUST returned from Edinburgh, another first for me. I had only passed through it before and admired the fairy castle in the sky. What a beautiful city: beautiful streets, squares and buildings, and magnificent trees (elms still flourish there). My reason for being there was the joyous occasion of the marriage of Andrew Gimson to Sally Malcolm-Smith, which went off splendidly. The bride wore white and a Paddington bear hat, rather than a veil. I've never seen that before. The reception was a great treat, as it was held in the very grand Signet Library opposite St Giles Cathedral. A truly great place for a beano, except of course there was no smoking allowed. So a band of us lepers were to be found lurking in the courtyard where the kind waitresses nevertheless brought us drinks.

I was staying with an old friend who is over seventy but never out of the kitchen. He stuffed me night and day with grouse, lobsters, crab and really good breads from the local bakery, not to mention a wonderful selection of cheeses. We also went to Whighams in Hope Street; one of John Noble's (he of the Loch Fyne fish and oysters) places for prawns and smoked haddock. It's situated in the wine vaults, which may be quaint but I found it so dark as to be very inconvenient.

My wedding companion was the red-bearded Christopher Howse, from the *Sunday Telegraph*, who is a boon to be with as he seems to know everything of interest. We went to a very, very strange mass on Sunday at the Catholic Cathedral which has startling sculpture by Eduardo Paolozzi outside. One is a giant foot bigger than a van. I can't think what it is for. There was not only a guitar player, but a trombone and drums. Their playing seemed to have nothing to do with the unknown, cowboy-type hymns and they sang the 'Our

Father' to the tune of 'This is a lovely way to spend an evening' – very unusual. The epistle was all about that fellow whose grapes grew sour which was referred to in the sermon by the priest asking 'What grape are you?', which gave me the giggles and Christopher got a dangerous *fou rire* when a little boy stated in pure Edinburgh accent, 'I'm a big fat juicy one.' What a lovely few days, I did enjoy them and must return.

7 January 1994

BY THE TIME you read this I hope we will all have had a splendid Christmas with little acrimony and lots of excitements, including wonderful midnight masses and carols. So I can now wish you all a lovely New Year. If all goes well I will have been in Barbon by Carnforth, staying with the estimable Dr John Martin Robinson, he of the Heralds and the Heritages. He has a ravishing 18th-century farmhouse with a privy outside which holds five bottoms. (Can you imagine the chitchat?) Luckily there are normal ones inside the house.

I had the curious duty of having to meet a friend at St Thomas's hospital who had just had a camera put down his throat. (Did you know that such patients are not allowed to leave unless they are met?) So I toddled along on my motorbike, picked him up and went off for a delicious lunch at his club, The Travellers. I love these gents clubs which seem to be run by very nice girls. I had smoked cod's roe to which I am addicted, a dear little partridge, and cheese. Very suitable I thought. The patient had soup, scrambled eggs, and semolina pudding – very nursery and again most suitable.

Meanwhile I have been recording some programmes for the BBC called *A Question of Taste* which are rather jolly food quizzes. The first one was at Ford (of open prison fame) near Arundel – I had no idea it was such a long and tedious journey. In the evening dusk the hotel looked like an old converted abbey, but was actually built in 1920 by Lord Moyne as a family house. My partner was Anthony Worall Thompson, and our foes were Oz Clark and Matthew Fort. The chairman was the charming Chris Kelly. Very nice audience. Then a dreadful journey back with a druggie who fell into the compartment muttering strange oaths and crouching in his seat. I asked if he was all right so he said he would kill me then leaped for the window. Luckily the door was locked so we dragged him back and left for another part of the train. Terrifying. The next port of call was Canterbury, where both Oz and Anthony had been to school. This time we had Robert Carrier as part of our team. He was in splendid form and is about to open a new restaurant in the spring having decided to return to Blighty for good, which, considering his abodes in Morocco, Paris and New York, shows we are not such a bad old country as people imagine. We returned by way of Faversham and this time had a magnificent dinner at a one-star restaurant called Reads, at Painter's Forstal – really enjoyable scallops, sea bass, oxtail, duck etc., and sumptuous little puddings. Bravo!

For a New Year's change, see if you can get some wild boar which is now bred in this country. (Otherwise you could use venison or hare, I suppose).

Cuissot de Marcassin Touraine

2 lbs of wild boar, deboned
8 oz of unsmoked streaky bacon
2 cloves of garlic
1 large onion
2 carrots
1 tablespoon of plain flour
4 tablespoons of brandy
Half a bottle of Chinon
Half a pint of good beef stock
Bouquet garni, salt and pepper

Slice the meat into two-inch chunks. Chop the bacon and slice the vegetables. Rapidly brown the boar in a little olive oil, remove from the pan with a slotted spoon. Cook the bacon in the pan, add the vegetables and stir in the flour until all is well mixed. Replace the boar with the other ingredients, pour over the brandy and flame. Finally, mix in the Chinon, beef stock, bouquet garni and season to taste. Transfer to a casserole and cook in a preheated oven at Gas 7, 425F, 218C, for about 1½ hours. The meat should be tender and the sauce a rich dark brown colour. Serve with buttered noodles or beautiful mashed potatoes and a good salad. Chinon, which is noted for its aroma of wild strawberries and crushed violets, is used because it retains its colour in a sauce, and is particularly good with red meats and game.

21 January 1994

I THINK I started being a godmother when I was about sixteen and since then have collected a quantity of godchildren spanning many generations. I feel I am now too old to be of any long-term use to an infant. However I have just become a godmother again (this must really be the last) to the beautiful daughter of Sara and Robert Toynbee-Towler, due to their persistence. She was baptised Madeline at the Church of Our Lady of Victories in Kensington High Street, and a very curious ceremony it was. I have not been to one of the new method baptisms before. I am used to holding the child over the font, but now it is left in the mother's arm – bit of a swiz, I felt. But it all went off splendidly, the devil got his comeuppance and we all repaired to the Towlers' house for a delicious lunch and lots of drink, surrounded by ravishing young parents and their spirited joyful children all dressed to kill and looking lovely. Unlike Nicholas Coleridge, I do not expect to fork out £3,000 for my duties. Another of my goddaughters, Sophie Hartman, cooked lunch on Christmas Day – watercress soup, salmon en croute, steamed vegetables and individual Christmas puddings, what could be better? – and such a relief! She also gave me some grand olive oil and balsamic vinegar. Now there is a good goddaughter for you.

I seem to have been to several posh hotels lately. Lunch at the Royal Garden Hotel in the Roof Restaurant, my goodness what a splendid view over London and all the surrounding parks! Worth going just for that, but the food was excellent and the Menu du Jour is a set £18.95. Unfortunately it is closing down soon for re-building.

We finished our quiz show, *Questions of Taste*, at the Four Seasons Hotel – rather a grim place I thought, cheerless and chandeliered. And finally a spiffing party at the good old Savoy. The cloakroom was full of exquisite young girls in the grandest of evening dresses, all talking pure cockney. They were heavenly;

Lord knows what they were up to – having a ball at any rate.

Here is a tasty little dish to set before a king and a nice light change from the heavier viands we have been consuming.

Breast of Chicken with Prosciutto and Mozzarella

4 boned chicken breasts
Salt and freshly ground black pepper
1 oz of unsalted butter
1 tablespoon of virgin olive oil
1 Mozzarella (buffalo if possible)
4 fresh sage leaves
2 oz of prosciutto di Parma
6 tablespoons of dry white wine or vermouth

Have the prosciutto sliced a little thicker than is usual. Slightly flatten the chicken breast with the dampened blade of a large knife. Season all over with the salt and pepper. Heat the oven to Gas 4, 359F, 180C. Heat the butter and oil in a large frying pan until the foam begins to subside. Place the chicken breasts in the pan, skin side down, and sauté until brown. Turn them over and sauté for a further five minutes. Transfer them to an ovenproof dish.

Slice the mozzarella into four pieces and place a slice on each chicken breast. Put a sage leaf on each slice and cover the whole with the slices of prosciutto cut to the size of each breast. If the prosciutto has been cut thinly, place equal shares on each piece of chicken.

Pour the wine into the frying pan and boil rapidly to reduce by half. Pour over the chicken. Cover the dish with its lid or foil and cook in the oven for about 15 minutes until the mozzarella begins to ooze out. Serve immediately. I think a rather sloppy puree of potatoes, made with half milk and half chicken stock as well as butter, goes very well with this dish; then just a tomato salad on the side.

4 March 1994

I HAVE BEEN to two requiems this week. The first was for the dearly beloved mother of the five McCoy brothers who run the Tontine hotel and restaurant at Staddlebridge, Yorkshire, which I wrote about in the summer. It took place at the modern Catholic cathedral in Middlesborough, a building hideous beyond belief, a wigwam of pale wood with a ghastly mural meaning nothing behind the altar. However the service and singing were full of gusto and general love, followed by a terrific wake back at the Tontine. Great log fires and groaning tables, dogs and splendid children running hither and thither, lovely children who actually talk to you with animation rather than grunting. A worthy, joyous party for the great Mary Clare McCoy.

The other requiem was at the London Oratory, a magnificent old fashioned tridentine mass sung most beautifully by the choir, full black and gold vestments, no addresses, then a mini-wake over the road at the Rembrandt. Give me a good requiem any day rather than these peculiar memorial services which are more like rather bad cabaret shows conducted by very bad actors.

From there I went on to a lunch given by Dan Farson for his new book *A Dry Ship to the Mountains*, at the French Pub in Dean Street. A very jolly affair in all but the food, which was filthy. I was very disappointed as I had heard good things of this little restaurant. Let us hope that this was just a bad day or that something had gone terribly wrong in the kitchen.

My latest find is a shortbread from a small family firm where everything is done by hand. The taste and texture are a sort of crumble heaven, so unlike those hard little oblongs we are used to. Apart from the traditional shortbread there are chocolate chip ones, stem ginger shapes, and they are working on a roasted peanut variety, when they can find the perfect peanut for the job. The firm is run by Anthony Laing, whose grandfather invented the digestive biscuit, so he is a dyed in the wool biscuit maker. The label is 'Shortbread House' and they can be found in the big department stores, the Conran shops and good delicatessens. Expensive but sheer delight.

Fine great mackerel are plentiful at the moment, and are also one of the cheapest fish going. Try them instead of salmon for a poor man's gravad lax.

Poor Man's Gravad Lax

2 large mackerel (about 1 lb each)
2 level tablespoons of sugar
3 level tablespoons of sea salt
2 level teaspoons of chopped dill, fresh or freeze dried.

Have the fish filleted but leave the skin on. Mix the other ingredients together and rub the fillets on both sides with the mixture leaving the surplus on the cut side. Stick the cut sides together and place in a shallow dish, cover with foil, place another dish on top filled with some sort of weights. Leave in a cool place for 24 hours. Drain well, scraping off any surplus mixture. Wrap in cling film and chill or even half freeze. When very firm with cold, slice down on the bias excluding the skin, as for smoked salmon. The slices should be very thin, almost transparent. Serve on a plate with brown bread and butter and the following sauce. Beat an egg yolk with 2 level tablespoons of Dijon mustard and a little sugar to taste – I like half a teaspoon – and a tablespoon of white wine vinegar. Now slowly beat in about 6 tablespoons of the oil of your choice as if you were making mayonnaise. Season with salt and freshly ground pepper, a squeeze of lemon juice and some more dill. Drink iced vodka. (It goes without saying, so I shall say it, the fish should be gloriously fresh.)

1 April 1994

A TERRIBLE ADVENTURE this week. My poor old uncle, who is over eighty but still in good fettle, went to visit one of his co-brethren of the Society of St Vincent de Paul who had been ailing. On arrival the man closed the door, put the chain on it and then proceeded to hold my uncle at knife-point for four hours explaining that he would have to kill him as otherwise my uncle would inform the police. Luckily he had a bottle of whisky from which he was taking copious draughts all the time, and finally slumped on the sofa and passed out. What an affair! Apparently he'd had these turns before but no one had seen fit to mention it. I trust they won't let him out too quickly this time.

Yesterday I travelled to Leeds to do a tasting of shop-bought taramasalatas for the *Food and Drink* programmme. British Rail was in its element. When we ordered breakfast, one of our company just wanted a piece of toast, but was told by the waiter that though they had toast they couldn't serve it by itself, as it wasn't on the tariff and the powers that be might think he had pocketed whatever was charged for it. A piece of toast is going to ruin the joint, I ask you! The Hot Breakfast Tray which consisted of cold omelette, potatoes which had not been sautéd as advertised, fat leathery bacon and spongy fatty chipolatas arrived with far too much soggy toast of which everyone left at least two slices. Dotty, dotty, dotty. Apart from that it was a good quick train.

We met the camera crew at the Olive Tree Greek Restaurant and were welcomed by the splendidly ebullient proprietor, George Psarias who kissed us all and pressed refreshments on us. He and I had to taste 12 different brands of taramasalata blind and I am glad to say that none of the great supermarkets won; that honour went to a Greek delicatessen store. I don't want too see or smell taramasalata for quite a while. I have discovered what that extraordinary pink colour you so often see in this product comes from. Beetroot. Why? Smoked cod's roe was never that colour and I think it looks deeply sinister. George then made his own version using salted cod's roe which again had this shocking pink overtone but the final product was very good. I still prefer the smoked roe's taste, though of course it is very expensive and I suppose difficult to find in some parts of the country. Also you need twice the amount of the smoked roe.

This is George's version:

Taramasalata

4 oz of crustless stale good white bread
3 oz of salted Tarama cod's roe or
6 oz of fresh smoked cod's roe
Juice of 1½ lemons
2 tablespoons of finely-chopped onion
10 fluid oz of light olive oil or vegetable oil

Soak the bread in water for 10 minutes then squeeze dry. Place in a food processor or blender. Skin the smoked roe and add this or the salted roe to the bread with the onion and a little of the lemon juice. Blend until smooth. Start adding the oil with the machine running, drop by drop to begin with as for mayonnaise, then in a steady thin stream. When thickish add the rest of the lemon juice. If it gets too thick dilute with cold water or more lemon juice, if too thin add more oil slowly. Taste and adjust to your liking. Refrigerate and garnish with flat parsley and black olives.

He also made hummus as follows:

Hummus

Soak 8 oz of dried chickpeas overnight. Drain and boil them in fresh water for one hour until tender. Remove any scum. Drain but reserve ½ pint of the liquid. Process the peas and the liquid with 2 fat cloves of garlic until it becomes a creamy paste. Add 2 tablespoons of tahini, 8 fluid oz of best olive oil, the juice of 1 or 2 lemons to taste and some rock salt. Mix thoroughly, adding more warm water if too thick. Keep tasting and adjust the seasoning, adding more lemon juice, garlic or salt. Place in a pretty bowl, dribble more olive oil over the top and dust with paprika. Sprinkle with chopped parsley and decorate with black olives. Refrigerate.

Serve both these dishes with hot pitta bread.

15 April 1994

WRITING AHEAD OF time, I hope we all had a fine and beautiful Easter, rolling eggs, hunting for eggs or giving eggs of the most sumptuous chocolate full of more sumptuous chocolates, but in all probability getting something nasty and brittle in fake milk chocolate looking like a bunny. If my foot improves I will have been in Yorkshire hoping for great and solemn services from the monks at Ampleforth but even there you can get some nasty new innovations. I managed to hobble to the *Evening Standard*'s literary lunch at the Dorchester, which was very entertaining as I sat between Paul Johnson who drew caricatures of everyone and Colin Haycraft who was being witty and mischievous about all comers.

The literary lions on show included the venerable Sir Stephen Spender, looking wonderfully handsome despite a recent illness; he has a magnificent head and flowing white hair, and has just had his ninetieth birthday. The others were Susan Crosland and the stalwart Sandy Gall, both elegant and pleasant. The show was masterfully minded by a very jolly A N Wilson and the lunchers seemed to be enjoying themselves to the full. Our lot ended up in the bar which was ravishing – just like a set from an Astaire and Rogers film, all chrome and bannisters.

If you are of a fiery temperament down to your tastebuds, Sainsbury's are now selling three new speciality varieties of chillies. Caribe, which is yellow, sweet and mild enough for salads, sauces and Mexican cooking. Anaheim is green and useful for stuffings and stews. Habanero is orange and hot with a distinctive fruit flavour and is ideal for soups and sauces.

If you are a health freak there is something extraordinary on offer called Sun Source Algae which grows wild in a pure mountain lake in Oregon. It seems to contain everything you might ever need including higher energy, mental clarity and a tremendous increase in emotional well-being. Who could resist? Available from Lambtons, 6 Rosenau Crescent, London SW11 (0171 223 1265). You drink it with fruit juice.

Back to basics; let us have a really good fish pudding from Pepita Aris's *The Spanishwoman's Kitchen* – real Basque fare.

Pink Souffléd Fish Pudding

1½ lbs of filletted white fish
1½ pints of fish stock, water and white wine (mixed)
½ a large onion, finely chopped
1 tablespoon of olive oil
2 garlic cloves, finely chopped
1½ lbs of ripe tomatoes, peeled and chopped
2 tablespoons of finely chopped parsley
½ teaspoon of sugar
Salt and fresh ground pepper
2 oz of butter
1 slice of stale white bread soaked in 2 tablespoons of milk
4 large egg yolks
3 large egg whites

Heat the stock, water and wine, slip in the fish (making sure it is covered).

When it comes to the boil, remove from the heat. Fry the onion and oil in a saucepan, when coloured add the garlic, tomatoes and parsley. Cook until thickened. Press through a sieve or blend and season with salt, pepper and sugar. Butter a 2½ pint bread tin with ½ oz of the butter, line with foil and butter again. Remove fish from the poaching liquid and shred with 2 forks, discarding skin and bones. Heat the butter in a wide saucepan and gently warm the fish, mixing in the crumbled bread. Add the tomato sauce, heat through, then beat in the egg yolks off the heat. Adjust seasoning. Whisk the egg whites with a pinch of salt to soft peaks then lightly fold in the fish mixture. Turn into the prepared tin. Stand in a small roasting tin and pour boiling water round to come ⅔rds up the sides of the bread tin. Cook in a preheated oven on Gas 4, 350 F, 180 C, for 50 minutes. Wait a moment or two, then run a knife round the pudding and turn out on to a dainty dish. Best served hot with a cream and parsley sauce but can also be eaten cold. Chill, slice and spread with a thin mayonnaise just before serving. Good for a picnic or travelling along the highway.

29 April 1994

I THOUGHT I was returning to London today but I have been inveigled into staying another couple of days in Yorkshire so here I am in the kitchen in front of a nice warm Aga trying to make an incredibly old typewriter behave properly. I came down here on Maundy Thursday, as far as York, where I had to find a man with two children on the platform. Of course I found no such thing, but tracked him down in the bar. We finally got to our destination in Ganthorpe Hall close by Castle Howard.

More and more folk kept arriving with cots and babies strapped about them until we settled down for Easter Sunday lunch with no less than 22 active human beings. We had gone to mass in a little church at Gilling belonging to the Ampleforth Prep School. Robert Towler brought his two small children along who had the triumph of ruining the entire service for all by screaming blue murder throughout, to such an extent that the kind Father Matthew from

Ampleforth interrupted the mass during the canon to proffer Easter eggs to the little wretches. He then very politely suggested they be banished from the scene.

But lunch was splendid. Roz Pennybacker, my hostess and Diana of the hunting fields, is one of those beautiful creatures who seems to have everything in hand and ready without any apparent effort or fuss. Not only preparing a vast amount of Pascal lamb to be devoured but laying a treasure hunt of Easter eggs all over the garden in between bastings.

They are incredibly tough these country folk. I have been to four large houses over the past few days and not one of them had the central heating turned on, especially now there is this terrible new VAT, but they don't seem to mind. I do. I go to bed in most of the clothes I have on, clutching a hot water bottle and lying in terror of the moment I have to broach the bathroom. I suppose it takes time to thicken the blood of us puny Londoners.

A great deal of proper eating goes on to combat the cold – full breakfasts and teas with muffins and cakes, so I think I will give you Roz's excellent, moist and dark ginger cake, which comes from her mother Jean Toynbee down the road.

Jean Toynbee's Ginger Cake

8 oz of self-raising flour
4 oz of soft brown sugar
2 eggs
½ teaspoon of bicarbonate of soda
1 dessertspoon of dry ginger powder
½ teaspoon of cinnamon
¼ pint of milk
4 tablespoons of black treacle
4 oz of butter or margarine

Mix all the dry ingredients together, having sieved the flour, ginger, bicarbonate and cinnamon to remove any lumps. In a saucepan, heat the butter, milk and treacle until melted together. Beat the eggs into the dry ingredients until thoroughly mixed and smooth, then mix in the treacle ingredients. If you have a processor the whole thing can be accomplished therein without any sieving. Pour the mixture into a greased baking tin and bake in a low to moderate preheated oven at about Gas 4, 350°F, 180°C for 45 minutes. This can be turned out, cooled and kept in a cake tin or, what is very delicious, served as a hot pudding with whipped or clotted cream and maybe some stem ginger in syrup if you have some handy.

27 May 1994

Farfalle with Fresh Peas and Mint

1 medium onion, peeled
4 fluid oz of extra virgin olive oil
4 slices of pancetta or bacon
1 clove of garlic, peeled and chopped
1 dried chilli pepper, crumbled
1 lb of fresh peas (shelled weight)
A good handful of fresh mint, washed and chopped
14 oz of farfalle pasta
4 oz of freshly grated parmesan cheese
Salt and freshly ground black pepper

SLICE THE ONION in half from end to end. Slice each hemisphere very thinly. Heat the olive oil and fry the diced pancetta briefly. Before it turns crisp, add the onion, garlic and chilli. Throw in the peas and mint. Season with salt and pepper, then cook very gently for 10-12 minutes while you boil the pasta. If you cannot find farfalle (pasta bows) substitute any of the other stubby pasts like fusilli, penne, shells, etc. Boil the pasta as usual in a large saucepan of fast boiling water, drain when al dente and mix thoroughly with the peas. Sprinkle with half the parmesan and serve immediately. The remaining cheese to be handed round in a bowl. I imagine this dish could be prepared perfectly successfully with good frozen peas and less cooking time.

How about a mint julep for cocktails? Why don't we have them here? So delicious, and we do have plenty of mint, but bourbon is expensive. If you have some by you, this is the receipt.

Mint Julep

4 teaspoons of caster sugar
12 ice cubes
A little water
12 sprigs of mint
Enough crushed ice to fill 4 tall glasses
5 fluid oz of bourbon

Frost 4 tall glasses by leaving them in the freezer for a short time. Put the sugar, the ice cubes and a splash of water into a jug. Stir to allow the ice to melt a little and the sugar to dissolve. Add half the mint to the jug. Fill the jug with the crushed ice and the bourbon. Stir around then divide the contents of the jug equally between the four frosted glasses. Decorate with the remaining mint. Cheers!

10 June 1994

I WENT TO an enchanting christening in Westminster Cathedral last Saturday and had to be a proxy godmother for the ravishing baby, Josephine Rose Lawson-Tancred. She was as good as gold and thoroughly delighted with the whole proceedings of becoming a card-carrying Christian Catholic.

Back to the house for a really expertly-managed barbecue executed by Alfredo, an Angolan Portuguese. Juicy pungent chunks of leg of lamb which had been marinating for days in heaven knows what, but the result was perfection. Of course it started to pour with rain which dispirited no one and the children got covered in black ashes and christening cake. Bliss.

I ended up returning to dinner with another part of the family, the Macaskie lot, who picked up a brace of duck at Lidgates to have another feast. I got bitten in the arm by a splendid rabbit with very long floppy ears who roams round the house like a fur muff. He is very handsome but not for the pot.

Safeways are producing oak-smoked mushrooms at £1.49 for a 125g pack,

which is about $4\frac{1}{2}$ oz, so rather expensive, but they are meant to go further in taste value than the ordinary ones. They are called Chislet mushrooms and according to the blurb are a great new ingredient for the witty cook. What on earth can they mean? The English asparagus should be £1.99/lb.

Daregal's individually quick frozen herbs from Frigifrance are another new idea. You keep them in the freezer and because they are coated in oil before being frozen you can shake and sprinkle them at will without defrosting them. They include dill, mint, garlic, shallots, various mixed herbs, parsley, coriander, thyme, chives, rosmary, basil and sage, but no tarragon I regret to say. However, try this dish incorporating them if you don't have the fresh ones.

Magrets de Canard avec les Petites Choux Farcis

(*Duck breasts with stuffed cabbage to you, dear*)

4 oz of peeled carrots, shredded
4 oz of white leek, shredded
4 oz of celery, shredded
2 oz of butter
Salt and fresh ground black pepper
8 large, good shaped cabbage leaves
1 teaspoon of Daregal quick frozen shallots
2 teaspoons of Daregal quick frozen thyme
4 trimmed duck breasts
4 small slices of French bread
Pâté for the bread
$\frac{1}{3}$ of a pint of red wine
$\frac{1}{2}$ pint of duck or chicken stock
2 tablespoons of redcurrant jelly
4 tablespoons of crème fraiche

Fry the carrots, leeks and celery gently in half the butter for 3 minutes. Season to taste. Blanche the cabbage leaves in boiling water and drain on a tea cloth. Divide the vegetable mixture into 4 equal portions and wrap each one tightly in 2 cabbage leaves, then wrap them again in lightly oiled foil. These can be prepared in advance the day before if you like. Heat remaining butter in a frying pan. Add shallots, thyme and place the duck breasts skin side up. Fry briskly for 1 minute. Remove the duck breasts to an oven-proof dish (skin side uppermost) and cook in a hot pre-heated oven at Gas 7, 425°F, 220°C for 7 minutes. Place the little cabbage parcels in the oven for the last 4 minutes of the duck cooking time.

Toast the French bread and spread with pâté, warm through in the oven. Take the duck breasts from the oven and keep warm on a dish. Deglaze the pan juices with the wine and stock, cooking briskly until reduced by half. Stir in the redcurrant jelly and crème fraiche and bubble for a further few minutes. Slice the duck breasts diagonally, spoon over the cooking juices and serve with the de-foiled cabbage parcels and the pâté toasts. New Jersey potatoes and an orange salad steeped in gin would be excellent partnering.

22 July 1994

I HAVE BEEN having a wild time with the media in the last two weeks. First of all a television documentary about people who ride motorbicycles which took place in my local market in Tatchbrook Street. The trouble and time these people take is quite extraordinary. Instead of remaining on the ground to get a tiny shot of me arriving in the market, they got permission from the surrounding flats to photograph from the highest point of the building, almost aerial, lugging all their paraphernalia up there. Whew! I wonder if they will use it. The rest was simple, just buying fruit from my beloved fruit and fish stalls, but it took a good three hours.

They then went on to Carnaby Street for the leather-clad, skull-and-crossboned brigade on their enormous bikes. Next I had to discuss jellies for Radio 4 with Simon Parkes of *Vogue*, a very nice young man who arrived in those wonderful old-fashioned long shorts. I found a charming quote from the great chef Alexis Soyer: 'Jellies are one of the most wholesome productions of cookery; they are slightly nourishing and fortifying without being exciting.' Very suitable diet for hooligans, I should think.

Then I wound up at the Dorchester doing the cookery quiz *A Question of Taste* with Chris Kelly in the chair. I was with Antony Worrall Thompson against Oz Clarke and his partner. It all got very out of hand and was great fun, like playing party games, and better still, we won by a whisker.

I have to do a fish salad for *Woman's Hour* so for a practice run try this one:

Warm Trout Salad with Orange Dressing

(*serves 4*)
2 lb of trout, cleaned
1 tablespoon of dry white wine
8 oz of asparagus or French beans
4 oz of mangetout or freshly cooked peas
8 oz of assorted salad leaves
A handful of watercress
4 spring onions, thinly sliced

Dressing:

4 tablespoons of Dijon mustard
4 tablespoons of olive oil
4 fluid oz of freshly-squeezed orange juice
The coarsely-grated zest of one orange
Salt and pepper

If you can't find a 2 lb trout get smaller ones to make up the same weight. Preheat the oven to Gas 6, 430F, 200C. Lay the trout on a lightly-oiled piece of kitchen foil, pour over the wine and wrap carefully, pinching the sides together. Place on a baking sheet and bake for 30 to 40 minutes depending on the sizes of the trout. Remove from the baking sheet and allow to cool in its wrapping of foil.

Blanch the asparagus or beans in boiling water for 3 minutes. Blanch the mangetout for 30 seconds. Drain, refresh under cold water, leave to cool and dry on a tea towel.

Combine the torn salad leaves (try to include some rocket) the watercress and the spring onions in a bowl. Grate the zest of one orange coarsely and mix with the orange juice. Mix in all the ingredients for the dressing. Season to taste with salt and a good deal of freshly ground pepper.

Remove the skin from the trout and flake the fish, discarding any bones. Add the asparagus and the mangetout to the salad leaves and mix with the dressing. Turn out onto a fine charger or flatish dish then arrange the flaked trout on top. Serve at once.

A scrumptious ice-cream for a summer's evening from Michael Lampton:

Frozen Leopard

12 oz of crumbled macaroons or amaretti
4 oz of caster sugar
4 fluid oz of single cream
4 fluid oz of brandy
12 fluid oz of double cream

Combine the biscuits and sugar then mix in the brandy and the single cream. Whip the double cream until it forms soft peaks and fold into the other ingredients. Freeze at will in a covered plastic box. Remove from freezer into refrigerator about ¾ of an hour before serving. What could be easier?

November 1994

HALLOWE'EN WILL BE over by the time you read this but that is no reason to forget the pumpkin for another whole year. We don't set much store on pumpkins, merely regarding them as decoration or suitable conveyance for Cinderella to get to the ball but all this is changed for me. Yesterday, one of those beautiful Indian summer days, I went with the BBC's *Food and Drink* programme to a ravishing little village called Slindon, near Arundel, to meet the pumpkin king, Mr Ralph Upton and his wife Barbara who live in Pumpkin Cottage.

They look like something out of a benign fairy tale and sell 20,000 pumpkins and squashes a year. People come from far and wide to stop and stare and purchase from this wondrous place. Great mountains of pumpkins and squashes, orange and gold, jade greens, stripes and creamy white skins are piled high to delight the eye. I've never seen anything more splendid in the vegetable kingdom. So many varieties and tastes from simple marrows to peppery patty-pans, chestnut-flavoured gourds, spaghetti marrows, hubbard squash (which some Americans from Brighton and Havant had come to buy their stocks of for the year). They also went for some small oval ones, maybe the uchiki kuri with its red flesh which they roast in the oven with brown sugar and bacon like Boston beans. There is a small black round one that looks like a little bomb. I boiled it in water without the instructions to pierce before cooking had reached me and on piercing it, it exploded with a huge bang, leaving orange strands all over the kitchen and a nasty burn on my hand. So take care, even Mrs Upton lost a saucepan lid for two weeks after one of these explosions. If you are anywhere near this amazing place, go and see for yourself – well worth a drive.

Try this receipt from Toulouse-Lautrec:

Gratin of Pumpkin

A 2lb piece of pumpkin, peeled, depipped and defibered
Seasoned flour
Oil
1 lb of onions sliced
8 oz of tomatoes, peeled, fresh or tinned
Salt, pepper, sugar
Breadcrumbs and butter

Slice the pumpkin into ½" by 3" pieces. Shake them in flour. Fry them in oil until golden, batch by batch, drain on kitchen towels. In another pan cook the onions gently in oil until soft but not browned, add the tomatoes and stew until you get a moist mixture sauce. Season with salt, pepper and a little sugar. In a gratin dish, layer the slices of pumpkin and the onion mixture adding a little extra seasoning. Finish with pumpkin and scatter it evenly with breadcrumbs. Melt an ounce or so of butter and drizzle it over the crumbs. Bake in oven at Gas 4, 350°F, 180°C, until bubbling round the sides, about 45 minutes. Finish browning the top under the grill. To make a change you could also add Gruyère cheese to the crumbs. Serve immediately.

March 1995

I HAD A very unusual experience earlier this month. I travelled to Exeter then on to Ottery St Mary to visit the wild boars being bred in the woods of Escot House, the Devon seat of the Kennaway family which they acquired in 1794. Captain John Kennaway was offered a Lordship for his services in India as recommended by the Marquis Cornwallis, but it is said that he refused the honour because it carried a standard of living beyond his means, so he accepted a baronetcy as a compromise.

Death duties have taken their toll since the First World War and much of the estate has been sold, the house needing repairs, etc, etc. The present incumbent, John-Michael, son of Sir John, has established an aquatic centre and garden, a pet centre, a restaurant converted from the lovely stables and mews and last but not least the wild boars in the wired-off forest enclosure, all to keep the place in good repair and funds. Good luck to him and his brave wife Lucy.

The boars were fascinating, charging about like small rhinos. The huge males, Millwall and Boris, are very frightening indeed, so much so that no-one enters their domain where they reign supreme, snorting, eating and begetting litters. The young boars being bred for the table were very amenable and were quite happy for us to be in their enclosure filming for the *Food and Drink* programme. We had a roasted wild boar shoulder for lunch which was delicious – rather brown and sticky like goose with a very fine flavour admirably set off by a wild cherry sauce.

We also tried a cross-breed of pork and boar called Eldon Wild Blue Pork which is bred in Hampshire – the best bit of pork I have had for years, with proper fat and crackling. Such luminaries as Pierre Koffman and Albert Roux dote on them. Try to get some – ask your butcher or write to Upper Eldon Farm, King's Somborne, Hants. Well worth the trouble.

I have received a splendid winter soup receipt from Carole Edlmann who lives in Estremoz, Portugal, where she assures me they often have freezing days. It is really a meal in itself.

Comforting Winter Soup

1 large onion, chopped
2 cloves of garlic, crushed
3 medium potatoes, diced
2 tablespoons of olive oil
4 oz of sliced green beans
1 tablespoon of thyme or oregano, chopped (½ if dried)
2 16 oz tins of red kidney beans
1 medium tin of chopped tomatoes (14 oz)
3 good quality thin Portugese or
Spanish chorizo sausages
3 good quality frankfurters
22 fluid oz of chicken stock
1 teaspoon of sugar
Generous dash of Worcester sauce
Black pepper and salt

Soften the onion in the olive oil, add the peeled, diced potatoes and stir for 2 minutes. Slice the sausages finely and add to the pan with the rest of the ingredients. Simmer for 30 minutes. Season with fresh ground pepper and salt if necessary. Serve with lots of hot crusty bread.

May 1995

I HAD TO make a so-called Easter cake for *Woman's Hour* but it was not to be a Simnel so I plumped for my favourite flavours and made a chocolate devil cake with coffee butter icing in the middle and pale coffee American frosting on the top, liberally dusted with fresh ground coffee and decorated with tiny speckled sugared chocolate eggs. It looked ravishing but it was for the wireless and no-one but my director, the strict Simon Parkes who insists that I don't cheat, could see it. He wanted to eat it at once which I forbade.

Then I spent three days filming for a television programme about veal and calves. They kept little of the cooking I did (making osso bucco) but a great deal of my careering about on my trusty motorbike. Funny lot, these media people.

I had a picnic lunch (an apple to be precise) at the *Catholic Herald* where the brilliant Cristina Odone had captured Tony Benn to give us a talk. He was very affable but seems to think that socialism still exists and made one wonderful statement to a room stuffed with Roman Catholics: 'I don't know what your views are on abortion, but... ' Great fun.

The spring lamb should be appearing, so I thought you might enjoy some different things to eat with it. These are from Richard Olney's new book, *A Provençal Table* (Pavilion Books).

Grilled Aubergines with Garlic Cream

4 plump heads of garlic, cloves separated and peeled
Salt and freshly ground pepper
About 4 fluid oz of olive oil
8 small elongated aubergines (about 4 lbs)

Cook the garlic in salted water at a slight boil for 12–15 minutes or until really tender. Drain them and push through a fine sieve. Season with salt and pepper and stir in enough olive oil to loosen the purée to a thin spreading consistency.

Cut off the stem ends from the aubergines and split each into two. With a sharp little pointed knife, make crisscross incisions on the cut surfaces. Dribble olive oil over the cut surfaces, smear it evenly around and season with salt and pepper. Grill the aubergine halves on a preheated grill, split surface first until golden brown, then finish grilling, skin side down until a knife tip meets no resistance near the stem end. Spread the crisscross surfaces with the warm garlic cream and serve with the lamb. Really good.

This can be a first course on its own, or a side dish

Potato Soufflé

(*serves 4*)
1 ½ lbs of potatoes, peeled and quartered
Salt
6 tablespoons of butter = 3 oz
8 fluid oz of milk, heated
Pepper and nutmeg
4 fluid oz of freshly grated Parmesan cheese
3 eggs separated
1 beaten egg yolk

Preheat the oven to Gas 6, 400°F, 190°C. Boil the potatoes in salted water until just done. Drain them and push through a sieve or a mouli into a suitable bowl. Stir in 5 tablespoons of butter cut into small pieces and enough hot milk to make a fairly loose purée. Season with salt and fresh ground pepper and a good scrape of nutmeg. Stir in the cheese.

Beat the 3 egg yolks with a fork and stir them into the potato mixture. Whisk the egg whites with a pinch of salt until they form soft peaks and fold them in gently with a wooden spoon. Empty the mixture into a generously buttered gratin dish and with a pastry brush paint the surface loosely with the other beaten egg yolk, spreading here and there with a knife blade. Bake for 20 to 25 minutes until golden and evenly swelled.

No hanging about with this dish, serve immediately. I find it goes very well with cold meats or poultry.

July 1995

I HAVE HAD another of my filming excursions, this time to Bakewell near Derby to discover the origin and correct version of Bakewell pudding (as opposed to tart which was a later development and is encased within short pastry). The pudding looks rather like an inverted mob-cap surrounded by its frill, which is produced by puff pastry. The filling is a layer of some good raspberry or straw-berry jam topped by a very rich mixture of egg yolks, butter and ground almonds and the all important 'secret ingredient', for which all three of the bakeries in Bakewell, claim to have the true and original receipt. Heaven knows what it might be: maybe it is just a mystery to keep people interested, I certainly couldn't discern it unless it was ratafia or almond essence.

We were there for three days with splendid weather until the last day which produced a sensational thunderstorm. But what a beautiful part of the world it is, with its two jewels of Chatsworth and Haddon Hall to stun the eye and gladden the heart.

Returning too late for shopping, I found nothing much to eat save a tin of tuna and a mysterious tin of smoked salmon soup (I can't imagine where it came from), the end of a bunch of celery going sinister around the edges and a solitary onion, so I used them all to make what turned out to be a curious but quite delicious soufflé. Try it if you are in the same sort of fix.

Odds and Ends Soufflé

1 tin of tuna (about 6-7 oz)
1 large onion
The same quantity of celery
1 tin of soup, mushroom would be fine
1 ½ oz of butter
1 tablespoon of plain flour
3 eggs and 1 extra white
Salt and fresh ground pepper
Grated parmesan

Melt butter in a saucepan large enough to contain all the ingredients. Chop the onion and celery and soften in the butter but do not brown. Stir in the flour and cook for a couple of minutes, stirring all the time, add the soup little by little and cook until you have a thick sauce.

Take off the heat, beat in the egg yolks one by one and mix in the tuna fish, separating the flakes. Leave to cool a bit.

Whisk the egg whites to a soft peak (if you don't have an extra white, don't worry – it's just that I always have a few lurking in the refrigerator). Stir a spoonful or two into the tuna mixture and season with salt and pepper, maybe a dash of Tabasco, then gently fold in the rest of the whites. Spoon mixture into a buttered soufflé dish, sprinkle with fresh grated parmesan and cook on a baking sheet in a pre-heated hot oven at gas 7, 425°F, 220°C for 25–30 minutes.

Now that summer has finally arrived, try these peaches from Raymond Blanc:

Stone 8 ripe peaches and place in a large saucepan. Add 1 pint of white wine, 7 oz of caster sugar, 1 vanilla pod and 4 sprigs of fresh mint. Cover with the finely sliced pieces of 1 orange and half a lemon. Put in enough water to barely cover the peaches. Bring to the boil, skim off any impurities, lower the heat to a very gentle simmer. Cook for 15 minutes then leave to cool in the syrup.

Transfer the peaches to a glass serving bowl arranging the fruit slices on top. Pour over the syrup and serve with some exquisite sweet biscuit like Cigarettes Russes.

October 1995

I VERY NEARLY massacred an entire film crew plus producer and director last week. I think it was the most frightening moment of my life. We were doing a film pilot and after a dangerous morning of shooting simulated rabbits and pheasants at the Holland and Holland shooting school the afternoon consisted of making me drive a 650cc motorbike and side-car. This is incredibly difficult, the side-car seems to take over and drag you to the wrong side of the road. The brave owner of the vehicle sat in the side-car and off we went. We veered into a ditch the first time but gradually, with a panting heart, I managed to control the beast. Then we shot the film with the courageous Clarissa Dickson Wright as my passenger. All went well until the last shot had to be done later in the day. I must have lost my cunning by then. I completely lost control of the machine's direction, hit the camera's very expensive tripod, careered away just in time and ended up hitting a flag post which mercifully stopped my progress. Clarissa was a brick and made no moan whilst staring death in the face. Ah me, what larks.

I arrived home to find that the New Covent Garden Soup Co had left two of their winter range soups on my doorstep, a good earthy Puy Lentil with thyme and an interesting Kohlrabi and Caraway one which I consumed cold with a dollop of créme fraîche.

I love Puy lentils (the tiny black ones): this receipt makes a good side dish or starter if you wish.

Marinated puy lentils

10 oz of Puy lentils
4 cloves of garlic
A big handful of fresh coriander
A big handful of flat parsley
8 fluid oz of good olive oil
4 oz of anchovies in olive oil
Rock salt and black pepper

Cook the lentils for about 15 minutes in boiling unsalted water until just cooked, maybe only 10 minutes depending on how fresh they are. Drain well. Using a pestle and mortar pound the the peeled garlic and anchovies with a

22
15
12
16

little salt rock into a paste. Add the olive oil slowly until all is mixed well. Heat this mixture over a low flame until it bubbles then stir in the lentils. Remove from the heat. Roughly chop the coriander and parsley and toss into the lentils. Season with ground salt and pepper. Serve with grilled sweet peppers, aubergines and cherry tomatoes. Shave some parmesan over the top. A ravishing dish to behold. It should be served at room temperature and improves if made about 6 hours before eating. Enough for four or five folk.

Try these fish cakes for a change of taste.

Smoked Trout Fishcake

(*serves 2*)

2 oz of trout fillet
2 oz of smoked trout
4 fluid oz of whipping cream
2 slices of good white bread soaked in milk
2 oz of mashed potato
Small bunch of parley or coriander, chopped
Salt and pepper
To breadcrumb: Flour, 1 beaten egg and 4 oz white breadcrumbs

Process the trout with the squeezed bread and the cream. Mix into the mashed potato, add the parsley or coriander and season to taste. Roll into balls using the flour on your hands. Chill. Flatten the balls into discs, dip into egg and breadcrumbs. Fry in a little oil and finish in the oven. For the sauce, boil together 2 fl oz lemon juice, 7 fl oz water, 2 oz caster sugar, 1 minced clove of garlic, 1 red chilli, deseeded and chopped, diluted cornflour or arrowroot to thicken (mix with a little water in a coffee cup and add when the rest comes to the boil, little by little to achieve a light consistency). Season at will. Arrange the fishcakes on a bed of stir fry vegetables and serve with the sauce.

January 1996

I AM NOT sure that I would be terribly flattered to have a potato named after me, however delicious it might be. A rose yes, but a potato? This is what Sainsbury's have done to the exquisite Anya Linden, one time ballet dancer and now married to the previous chairman John Sainsbury. Anya is a nice waxy salad potato with pale pink skin and white flesh (that's complimentary I suppose), bred from the Pink Fir Apple, retaining the flavour but getting rid of the 'knobbly' bits (thank heavens for that). It is a very good thing that more interest is being shown in the different varieties of the spud. Sainsbury's now boast 40 of them to choose from at various times of the year.

I was having a splendid Sunday lunch with proper pork that had real crackling and what I thought was going to be red cabbage – but it wasn't. It was onions which Sara Toynbee had cooked from a receipt of Alastair Little (she said, but it is not in my book). Here is her delicious rendering of it.

Onions Stewed in Red Wine

3 lbs of onions
2 oz of butter
1 tablespoon of soft brown sugar
Salt and pepper
16 fluid oz of hearty red wine
8 fluid oz of red wine vinegar
1 tablespoon of fresh thyme or ½ of dried
1 tablespoon of Cassis

Peel and slice the onions. Melt the butter in a large enough pan to contain all the ingredients then fry the onions gently for 5 minutes. Season with salt and freshly ground pepper, stir in the sugar and fry for a further 5 minutes. Now pour in the wine which will leave plenty in the bottle for you to have a nip, then add the vinegar and the thyme. Simmer very gently for about 1½ hours until nearly all the liquid has gone. Adjust the seasoning and add the Cassis if you have some. (Do not use Ribena, it just ain't the same.) This lovely dark red mess went beautifully with the pork, as it would with ham, tongue, or practically any roast.

Having mentioned Mr Little, have you ever tried his Danish omlette or as they call it in Denmark, egg cake. A most excellent supper dish.

Danish Egg Cake

4 slices of streaky bacon or speck
1 tomato or 3 cherry tomatoes
1 tablespoon of sunflower oil
3 eggs
1 tablespoon of double cream (optional)
1½ oz of butter
handful of chives
1 oz of smoked eel fillet (optional)

Preheat the oven to Gas 6, 400°F, 200°C. Cut the rind off the bacon and place the rashers on a rack in a roasting pan in the oven until it just begins to crisp. Remove from the oven and reserve. (This is a much better way of cooking bacon than frying or grilling.) Reduce the oven to Gas 3, 325°F, 160°C.

Brush your omlette pan with a little sunflower oil. Beat the eggs in a bowl with a little salt and pepper and the cream, if using, until just amalgamated. Do not overbeat. Put the pan over a meduim heat, add butter and swirl it around. Tip in the eggs, which will start to set immediately. Using a spatula push the egg away from the edges, leave for 60 seconds then repeat the process. Turn down the heat and cook very gently for 3 minutes until the bottom is set and lightly browned. If you have made a much larger cake and it still seems liquid put it into the cooler oven for 4 minutes. While the eggs are cooking return the bacon to the oven to warm through.

To serve, arrange the tomatoes cut in chunks round the edge of the pan, cut the bacon into ¼ inch pieces and use them to cover the top of the cake. Scatter with chopped chives and chopped eel fillet, if using. The cooking of this dish may require a little practise to achieve a layered effect of lightly browned egg and moist creamy egg. The cake can be made as individual omlettes with the quantities I have given above or in a large serving, in which case the pan is brought to the table and people help themselves to thick wedges. Eat with some good rustic bread and quaff Danish beer.

February 1996

HAVING HAD MY motor bicycle stolen before Christmas I have been lying doggo for a month until the arrival of a new one which I got last week. A proud beauty in red and white, named Ruby III, she was blessed by Father Ronald at the London Oratory. So let's hope that will keep her safe from dirty little malefactors.

Here is a splendid rich chocolate pie from Wales. You could bake it in one of those heart-shaped tins to wish your beloved a blissful St Valentine's Day.

Rich Chocolate Pie

For the pastry:
6 oz of plain flour
1 oz of cocoa (the real stuff)
2 tablespoons of icing sugar
4 oz of unsalted butter, diced
1 tablespoon of cold water

For the filling:
8 egg yolks
5 oz of icing sugar
6 level tablespoons of cocoa powder
12 fluid oz of double cream
12 oz of bitter chocolate
3 oz of unsalted butter
6 egg whites

To make the pastry, put all the ingredients into a food processor and whisk until the mixture forms a ball. Remove the ball and wrap in cling film. Chill in the refrigerator for 30 minutes. Roll out and line a 12 inch tin. Bake in a medium pre-heated oven at gas 4, 350°F, 180°C, for 15 minutes. Remove and allow to cool. For the filling, melt the bitter chocolate with the butter in a bowl over a pan of hot water then remove and leave to cool. Whisk the egg yolks and the icing sugar (add the sugar little by little or it blows all over the place) until they are creamy. Add the cocoa powder and whisk until thoroughly blended. Whip the double cream to a soft peak consistency and fold into the mixture then fold in the cooled melted chocolate. Whisk the egg whites until stiff and fold them into the chocolate mixture (start with quite a big bowl to receive all these ingredients). Pour the mixture into the pastry case and chill thoroughly. Remove from the refrigerator half an hour before serving. Decorate with more whipped cream flavoured with honey and whiskey to taste. What more could a heart desire? This gorgeous confection comes from Mary Ann Gilchrist.

Something quite the opposite in richness but fresh and toothsome nevertheless:

Watercress Dipping Sauce

Have a bowl of iced water at the ready. Bring a saucepan of water to a furious boil and stir in a trimmed bunch of watercress for 10 seconds on the boil then drain immediately and plunge into the iced water until quite cooled. Drain well and squeeze out as much liquid as you can with your dainty hands. Place in a food processor together with two spring onions, green stems as well, roughly chopped. Eight fluid ounces of soured cream, half a tea-spoon each of salt, lemon juice and tabasco or the like. Whizz until quite smooth. Adjust the seasoning to your taste and serve with crudities.

May 1996

I HAVE PASSED my motor cycle test for the second time and am now learning how to control a side-car attached to a 900cc Triumph for a forthcoming attraction (we hope) on the television. After several hours of painful practise in the bowels of Harlow, I ate my first McDonald's 'Big Mac' in a ghastly emporium full of children. I have never eaten anything so disgusting – three bits of some unidentifiable soggy bun, stuck together with hard little discs of supposed meat and a terrible plastic square of cheese, all completley tasteless. Perhaps that is their appeal.

Then I was taken to a really superb lunch at the Four Seasons restaurant in the hotel of the same name. A brochette of scallops, langoustines and various seafoods served in a beetroot oil (which I had never heard of) was a triumph,

followed by a succulent, gamey rabbit and to top it all a killer pudding which was a hot chocolate steamed mould filled with really good dark melted chocolate and served with a white chocolate ice-cream. A double whammy – a moment in the mouth, a month on the hips.

I have also discovered a Chocolate Club which will send ambrosia to your door. If you would like the outrageous catalogue or the opportunity to sample 'The Chocolate Club Range', you can contact Edwin Sheppard on 0171 384 1833. All their chocolates from around the world are made with 70 per cent cocoa solids, the real thing.

I suppose people are veering away from beef, not that I have noticed it, but I do hope that more attention is being paid to the quality of any meat purchased. Try this with the new lamb arriving shortly:

Garlic & Rosemary Rack of Lamb

With a rich redcurrant sauce

2 x 1lb racks of lamb (Welsh is excellent)
2 fresh sprigs of rosemary
2 cloves of garlic crushed roughly
2 tablespoons of red currant jelly with port – melted
1 tablespoon of plain flour
½ pint of lamb stock
2 tablespoons of crème de cassis or port (optional)

Place one rack of lamb fat side down, spread the garlic along the 'eye' of the meat and the rosemary sprigs on top. Place the other rack on top, fat side uppermost and interleaf the bones to make a guard of honour. Secure with fine string and place upright in a roasting tin in a pre-heated oven at Gas 6, 400°F, 200°C, for 30 minutes. Remove from the oven and brush with half the melted jelly. Return to the oven for 15–30 minutes depending on how pink you like it. Remove from the heat, cover in foil and let it rest for 15 minutes on a warmed dish. Drain the obvious fat from the roasting tin, heat the juices and stir in the flour, cook for 1 minute. Gradually add the stock and the remainder of the jelly. Stir for 2–3 minutes until thickened then add the crème de cassis or port at will. Slice the rack between the bones and serve with the rich redcurrant sauce, some new potatoes sprinkled with mint and something fresh and green.

For pork chops as a change from grilled, have:

Pork with Apple/Sultana Sauce

2 teaspoons unsalted butter
2 teaspoons of ground nut oil
For the sauce:
2 large cooking apples
1 oz sultanas soaked overnight in 2 tablespoons of cider
4 tablspoons of cider
Juice of 1 lemon

Season chops with salt and fresh ground pepper. Heat butter and oil in a roasting pan and brown the chops briskly for 2 minutes each side. Roast in a preheated oven Gas 5, 375°F, 190°C, for about 20 minutes, turning them over after 10 minutes. Peel, core and slice the apples. Place in a saucepan with the lemon juice and the 4 spoons of cider. Cook gently until the apples turn into a sauce-like consistency. Add the sultanas at the last minute. Serve with the pork chops and whatever you deem suitable.

June 1996

I HAVE ALWAYS wanted to go to a Cornish fishing harbour and at last I have had my wish. I spent a week filming in Mevagissey, the largest village on St Austell Bay. It was all I had imagined, bar a smuggler or two: wonderful rocky coves, beautiful scenery and amazing, amusing fishermen who couldn't have been kinder and more helpful to us in the quest for crabs and lobsters, fish and fishermen's tales. We took over the Sharksfin Hotel and its kitchens, bang on the harbour wall, stayed there, cooked there and were treated with utmost kindess by all. It rained non-stop but must be a joy in the sunshine, which deigned to arrive as we left.

Did you know that the word 'avocado' comes from the fruit's Aztec name *ahuacatl* which is a shortened version of 'testicle tree' – partly attributed to the shape of the fruit as well as its reputation as an aphrodisiac? When the Spanish discovered the fruit in the 16th century, they delicately substituted their similar-sounding word avocado, meaning lawyer. Well, there's a piece of breakfast information for you. I always thought of them as celestial butter. Try this hash from Antony Worrall Thompson.

Salmon Hash with Crispy Bacon & Avocado

(*serves 4*)

1 small red onion, finely diced
1 red pepper, seeded and finely diced
2 medium waxy potatoes, peeled and finely diced
3 tablespoons of dill, finely chopped
8 oz tin of Alaska salmon, drained
2 tablespoons of dill, finely chopped
Salt and fresh ground black pepper
4 eggs lightly beaten
8 rashers of bacon
2 avocados
2 teaspoons of lemon juice
Crème fraîche – about 2 fluid oz

In a non-stick frying pan (preferably) cook the onion, red pepper and potato in some of the olive oil until tender and just browning. Transfer to a mixing bowl. Flake in the salmon (I should use fresh salmon if you happen to have some left over) and the dill. Season to taste and allow to cool for a few minutes. Add the eggs to the bowl and combine thoroughly. In the same frying pan, heat the remaining olive oil. Spoon in the mixture to cover the whole pan. Allow to cook over a medium heat for about 5 minutes until browned underneath then turn it over and brown the other side. Meanwhile grill the bacon rashers until crisp. Skin and mash the avocados with the lemon juice. To serve, cut the hash into 4 wedges. Put dollops of crème fraîche on the side, a helping of avocado and the crisp bacon. An excellent combination.

There is plenty of fine fresh spinach about now. This makes a lovely little dish:

Spinach & Egg Ramekins

(*serves 6*)
1 oz butter
8 oz of cooked, chopped fresh spinach
1 small onion or 2 shallots, chopped
4 oz grated cheddar or parmesan cheese
6 eggs
5 fluid oz of double cream
1 clove of garlic
Salt, pepper, nutmeg

Melt the butter in a frying pan and sauté the onion or shallots until soft. Transfer to a bowl, mix in the spinach and season with the salt, fresh ground pepper and a good scrape of nutmeg to taste. Butter 6 ramekins. Put equal amounts of the spinach mixture into each pot. Top with 1 egg each. Peel and crush the garlic and add to the double cream, stir well and pour over each egg a fair amount. Sprinkle with the grated cheese. Stand the ramekins in a roasting tin half full of boiling water and bake in a pre-heated oven at Gas 4, 350°F, 180°C, for 15–20 minutes. Try not to overcook – the yolks should still be soft and they will continue cooking in their pots while you are getting them out to serve. Have some good hot bread or toast to go with them.

Note: to achieve 8 oz of cooked spinach, you probably need 1½ lb of raw spinach.

July 1996

I FOUND THE most wonderul butcher whilst filming in Cirencester, Jessie Smith by name, an Aladdin's cave of splendid beef with good thick yellow fat covering the great joints, properly hung and marbled throughout with seams of fat. Imagine the gorgeous dripping it would produce. Succulent sweetbreads, pink livers, and even good old fashioned faggots. Most of this produce came from the Prince of Wales' farms in the glorious Highgrove area. Lucky old Cirencester.

We had the motorbike and sidecar blessed at the London Oratory by dear Father Ronald, followed by a delicious lunch over the road at St Quentin's Brasserie. Very good value, £10 for the set lunch. The two gents at the next table left large glasses of armagnac which my director pinched, only to find that they had merely popped out to watch a fly-past. Poor Patricia had to own up – beautifully embarrassing. The gents couldn't have taken it better and we all became firm friends.

I am delighted to see that Grub Street have reprinted Margaret Costa's *Four Seasons* cookery book (£17.99). She was a heavenly person, as was her husband. They owned and ran Lacy's restaurant in Whitfield Street during the 70s which was one of the best of its time. As raspberries will soon be here I shall remember her:

Russian Raspberry Pudding

1 lb of raspberries
3 tablespoons of caster sugar
½ pint of soured cream
2 eggs
1 tablespoon of flour
More sugar to decorate

Turn the raspberries into a shallow, oval gratin dish and sprinkle them with 2 tablespoons of the sugar. Stand the dish in the middle of a slow oven, Gas 2, 300°F, 150°C, until the raspberries are hot through. Beat up the soured cream with the eggs, the flour and the remaining tablespoon of sugar. Pour the mixture over the raspberries and put it back in the oven at the same heat but nearer the top. Cook until the topping is pale golden brown and firm to the touch, about 45 minutes. Sprinkle with a little more sugar before serving. This can be served hot or cold. Hot, it smells absolutely delicious and is one of the nicest ways of eating raspberries.

A fine cold dish for the summer is:

Caponata Siciliana

4 largish aubergines, salt
8 anchovy fillets
1 head of celery, 1 large onion, 4 oz of black olives
¼ pint of tomato purée made from fresh or tinned tomatoes
2 tablespoons of sugar, ¼ pint of wine vinegar
1½ oz capers
1 7oz tin of tuna fish
2 tablespoons of chopped parsley
Black pepper
Olive oil

Peel and dice the aubergines, sprinkle with salt and leave to drain for an hour in a colander. Press out any moisture and fry in hot olive oil until soft. Soak the anchovies in warm water, blanch and chop the celery, slice the onion and stone the olives. Cook the onion in a little hot olive oil until very soft then stir in the tomato puree and the sugar. Cook for a little longer until the mixture is thick and dark in colour, stir in the vinegar. Simmer for 5 minutes then add the celery, olives, aubergines, the capers, diced anchovies, the flaked tuna fish and the parsley. Season to taste. Pile high in a rustic dish. Make well in advance and serve cold.

November 1996

I HAVE BEEN having a wild old time since last month, what with the beginning of our TV series and filming the last two episodes in Northumberland and Scotland. At the beautiful Kielder Water we cooked for 25 scouts who were perfectly charming and lit fires for us. We found magnificent mushrooms to eat (as well as deadly ones with their warning red caps) and were practically eaten to death by midges. We shot on a grouse moor and cooked all manner of game at Lennox Love, one of the Duke of Hamilton's houses outside Edinburgh. Great fun with an enormous, kilted piper playing round the dinner table in the hall for the tartan-clad guests. We had a fine time whirling about the beautiful Scottish countryside in our motorbike and sidecar. No crashes to my credit, thank goodness.

Sainsbury's have produced a new reduced sodium white bread, for those who wish to cut their salt intake, and a new range of 'Occasions' food for drinks parties: titbits such as mini prawn fishcakes, coronation chicken filos, salmon pesto and parmesan tartlets and others to reduce the time factor in your own kitchen. Rather useful. Safeways have a new wine selection guide and something lovely for the children – or weirdos – chocolate body paint with its own paint brush. What next?

Here is the prize-winning Stilton Sandwich of the year, won by The Cafe at Heal's:

Stilton with Crisp Bacon, Watercress & Pear Butter on Walnut Bread

2 oz of Stilton, crumbled
2 rashers of bacon, cut up and fried until crisp
½ bunch of watercress, washed and de-stalked
2 slices of good quality walnut bread
Farmhouse butter, softened
¼ of a ripe pear, puréed
Dash of lemon juice

Mix pear, lemon juice and butter in a blender. Leave for a few hours in the refrigerator. To assemble the sandwich, butter bread with pear butter, add watercress, then bacon. Top with the Stilton. Season with freshly ground black pepper and add the second slice of bread. Slice as desired.

Rosemary Skewered Lamb

1 lb lamb neck fillet, trimmed and cut into even dice
8 branches of fresh rosemary, 6 in. long or
8 skewers and ½ teaspoon of dry rosemary
2 tablespoons of olive oil
1 garlic clove, crushed
Juice of 1 lemon
3 small different coloured peppers, deseeded and sliced
2 oz sugar snap peas, trimmed
4 oz button mushrooms, halved
1 carrot, cut into sticks
1 bunch of spring onions, trimmed and sliced
1 tablespoon of dry sherry
2 tablespoons of soy sauce
8 oz medium thread noodles

Using a sharp knife remove all leaves apart from 1½ inches at the tip of each rosemary branch. Thread the lamb cubes onto the rosemary skewers. In a shallow dish mix together 1 tablespoon of the oil, garlic, lemon juice (and dried rosemary if using). Put the meated skewers into the dish, coat with marinade and leave for 10 minutes. Cook under a medium grill for 10 minutes, turning frequently and basting with marinade. Cook the noodles. In a wok or frying pan heat the remaining oil. Stir fry the vegetables, adding the sherry and soy sauce. Keep nice and crisp. Place noodles on a warm dish with the skewers of meat resting on top. Surround with the vegetables. This is a reasonably-priced dish, especially if you use New Zealand lamb. Do make sure it is properly thawed.

December 1996

I HAVE JUST had a very wild month what with the advent of our *Two Fat Ladies* on the television, two *Oldie* Literary Lunches at Simpsons-in-the-Strand, book signings in Newbury, Manchester, Liberty's and Waterstones in Leadenhall Market where I had never been, to my shame. Heavenly place, where we purchased some very good fish and game. We addressed the Carnivore's Club, went to the Food Fair at Olympia and appeared on two morning TV shows. I modelled outsize clothes for a new magazine, *Encore*, at a breakfast in the Groucho Club and lunched at The Oxo Tower, Mosimann, Marco Pierre White, San Lorenzo and The Collection, not to mention parties at the Oriental Club, The Reform Club and Bernard Quaritch the antique booksellers. I am now exhausted and even fatter and should be sent off to a health farm. It has all been great fun and we are getting another series. Hurrah!

I received a goodie parcel from a firm called The Merchant Gourmet containing a jar of Dulce de Leche which is like the caramel on the bottom of Banofie pie and originally came from Argentina. It can be used as a spread or in trifles, Banofie pie, meringues or spooned over ice cream. There were also vacuum packed chestnuts from France and chestnut purée which can be used in soups, pâtés or with sausage meat for a stuffing. All these excellent things can be found in major supermarkets and department stores. Try this delicious concoction.

Caramel & Ginger Ice-cream Parfait

1¾ pints soft scoop vanilla ice cream
2 oz meringues
1 oz stem ginger, finely chopped
11 oz Dulce de Leche

Line a 2pt loaf tin with cling film. Put the ice cream in a bowl and break up with a fork. Break meringues into small pieces and add to the ice cream with the ginger. Fold together but do not over-work the mixture too much, as the ice cream will melt. Fold in the Dulce de Leche, then transfer to the loaf tin. Quickly level then place in the freezer until firm. To serve, turn out of the tin, discard cling film and slice. Serve with fresh fruit such as strawberries, raspberries or peaches.

Now for something completely different:

Fish & Vegetable Roast

5 tbs clear honey or maple syrup
2 tsps wholegrain mustard
1 lb white fish cut into chunks
1 red pepper, deseeded and roughly chopped
12 oz salad potatoes, quartered
2 courgettes cut into chunks
1 aubergine, ditto
1 red onion, likewise
2 tomatoes, quartered
4 tbs olive oil
Juice of half a lemon
3 cloves garlic, crushed
Salt and fresh ground black pepper

Pre-heat oven to Gas 6/400F/200C. Mix honey and mustard then stir in fish. Cover and place in refrigerator. Place vegetables in a large roasting dish. Mix oil, lemon juice, garlic and seasoning. Pour over veg and mix until they are coated. Roast 35 mins, turning once, until the potatoes are nearly done. Add fish and marinade, mix well into veg and cook for 10-15 mins until fish is just cooked.

To make a quick hors d'oeuvres, how about good old Chopped Liver?

Sauté 1 diced onion and 1lb trimmed chicken livers in 2oz butter until livers are just pink inside. Chop finely with 4 hard-boiled eggs, small bunch of parsley, salt and fresh ground pepper. Press into a suitable container and refrigerate for at least 5 hours. Serve with matzo biscuits and dill pickle.

N88
TFL